In Spirit and Truth

In Spirit and Truth

A Vision of Episcopal Worship

EDITED BY

Stephanie Budwey,
Kevin Moroney,
Sylvia Sweeney, and
Samuel Torvend

Copyright © 2020 by Stephanie Budwey, Kevin Moroney, Sylvia Sweeney, and Samuel Torvend

All rights reserved. No part of this book may be reproduced, stored in a retrieval system, or transmitted in any form or by any means, electronic or mechanical, including photocopying, recording, or otherwise, without the written permission of the publisher.

Unless otherwise noted, the Scripture quotations are from New Revised Standard Version Bible, copyright © 1989 National Council of the Churches of Christ in the United States of America. Used by permission. All rights reserved worldwide.

Church Publishing
19 East 34th Street
New York, NY 10016
www.churchpublishing.org

Cover design by Jennifer Kopec, 2Pug Design
Typeset by PerfecType, Nashville, Tennessee

A record of this book is available from the Library of Congress.

ISBN: 978-1-64065-298-9 (paperback)
ISBN: 978-1-64065-299-6 (ebook)

Contents

Introduction	vii
A068 Plan for the Revision of the Book of Common Prayer	xi
1. Changing to Remain the Same: The Evolving Prayer Book Tradition *Jeffrey D. Lee*	1
2. Liturgy for Mission: An Interpretation of Resolution A0681 *Kevin J. Moroney*	13
3. Common Prayer, a Strong Thread *Kathryn A. Rickert*	25
4. The Episcopal Church: So Much More than a National Church *Sylvia Sweeney*	37
5. Diversity and Common Worship *Ruth A. Meyers*	47
6. Can Anglican Liturgy Be Universal? *Juan M. C. Oliver*	59
7. Initiated but Unfinished: Catechetical Foundations for Fine-Tuning the Baptismal Rite *William H. Petersen*	73

8. Baptism and Ordination in the BCP 1979   87
   Elise A. Feyerherm

9. On the Integrity of Eucharistic Communion   97
   Louis Weil

10. What Episcopalians Can Learn from Our Lutheran Communion Partners about the Composition of Eucharistic Prayers   109
    James Farwell

11. Rites of Healing and Transition in the Baptized Life: New Pastoral Orders in a new Prayer Book   123
    Susan Marie Smith

12. Welcoming Care of God's Creation in Liturgical Reform   135
    Samuel Torvend

13. Praying the Present and Future   145
    Kay Sylvester

14. "What We Think Is New Is in Fact Very Old!"   157
    Stephanie A. Budwey

15. Very Members Incorporate: Expansive Common Prayer   169
    Cameron Partridge

References   181

Contributors   189

Introduction

IN SPIRIT AND TRUTH has been a labor of love collaboratively created by the Anglican Colloquium of the North American Academy of Liturgy, a community of Anglican scholars who meet annually to discuss the liturgical life of our Anglican and Episcopal Churches. This group of scholars have spent their adult lives studying and often teaching about the nature of liturgy in a changing world. Trained in liturgical history, liturgical theology, and many also in the field of ritual studies, the colloquium has tremendous wisdom to offer the Episcopal Church as we move toward a new period of liturgical revision. Deeply convinced that the worship life of our churches is central to the life of faith and the mission of the church, these scholars give their lives to the work of encouraging meaningful, life-giving worship across the numerous denominations we represent.

When the colloquium gathered in January 2019, we heard a significant report from two of our members who are currently serving on the Episcopal Church's Task Force on Liturgical and Prayer Book Revision, the Rev. Dr. Ruth Meyers of Church Divinity School of the Pacific, and the Rev. Dr. Kevin Moroney of General Seminary. The task force was created by the 2018 General Convention and has been tasked with leading the church forward in sound liturgical revision processes that are both deeply respectful of our Anglican and Episcopal liturgical traditions and also allow us to address needs for other liturgical resources for the twenty-first century.

As the colloquium discussed the work before the task force and the critical role that congregations and dioceses would play in gathering new and revised rites, it became clear to us that one element not addressed by Resolution A068 of General Convention, but absolutely critical to the success of liturgical revision efforts, was the role adequate formation plays in preparing individuals and communities for revision. Our knowledge of the history of the development of the 1979 Book of Common Prayer illustrated how necessary education and formation were to positive reception of a new prayer book. In other words, we learned that it does not work to abruptly impose new rites on communities when the goal is true and transformative liturgical revision. True liturgical revision gives worshippers the time, space, and capacity to embrace a new prayer language for their personal and communal lives. If we want Episcopalians to embrace new liturgies, we must first invite them to see the need for new rites. We must invite those who have prayed with our 1979 rites and may anticipate praying with new liturgies into an open conversation that then shapes the direction our worship life will move in response to our current historical, social, and religious context. Effective formation involves providing needed information, engaging in dialog around issues that people are passionate about, and allowing experience coupled with conversation to form and perhaps reform perspectives, attitudes, and postures in worship.

As a group of scholars, many of whom teach or have taught in seminaries, the colloquium recognized its somewhat unique ability to support the work of the task force by offering educational resources that the task force had not been mandated to create or disseminate. At that January 2019 meeting the colloquium began to map out a process by which its members and others with special expertise in liturgy could provide educational resources for the church. This volume of essays directly related to aspects of the resolution that created and mandated the task force was our way forward. Through the variety of essays, with their discussion questions and suggested bibliography for more in-depth reading, our goal was to provide churches with tools for intelligent, cogent, accessible historical and theological conversation illuminating the liturgical revision envisioned in resolution A068. We believe that Episcopalians will be much more likely to embrace liturgical revision if they have an opportunity to understand the priorities General Convention emphasized in its call for revision before they are asked to pray with these revised liturgies.

Nancy Bryan of Church Publishing Incorporated, a longtime colloquium member, offered the possibility of turning these articles into a book that could be used as a Christian formation resource by Episcopalians across the church. She chose an editorial board of the Rev. Dr. Kevin Moroney (of General Seminary and also a member of the task force), Dr. Stephanie Budwey (of Vanderbilt Divinity School), the Rev. Dr. Samuel Torvend, (a parish priest and historian at Pacific Lutheran University), the Rev. Dr. Sylvia Sweeney (of Bloy House and the convener of the colloquium), and herself. The goal was to have our work completed in time for the colloquium's January 2020 gathering so that in addition to offering this resource to the church, we could use it as a starter for further academic conversations about liturgical revision.

We hope that churches across the country will now use this book and its discussion questions to begin the long and important process of preparing for liturgical revision. While it is too early to know exactly where those revisions will lead us, there are some things we can know already based upon the resolution. We know that the beauty and eloquence of the 1979 Book of Common Prayer will continue to be cherished by our church; that we are committed to moving more fully and consciously into a lived understanding of the centrality of our baptismal faith identity to every aspect of our Christian life and church's governance; that we remain committed to being a eucharistically centered worshipping community. We know that our authorized rites must be more linguistically and culturally accessible to those in the Episcopal Church who do not pray in English. We know that there must be new rites or adaptations of old rites that respond to pressing issues of inclusion and diversity. We know that there is need for a deeper expression of our human limits and responsibilities as created beings situated within God's expansive, blessed, and beloved creation.

With a shared understanding of our deepest held Christian values, we look forward to what the future brings for our worship lives and our missional lives as bearers of Christ to a troubled and broken world. May you be as blessed in your conversations growing out of this resource as we have been in ours.

Sylvia Sweeney, convener
Anglican colloquium, North American Academy of Liturgy

A068 Plan for the Revision of the Book of Common Prayer

RESOLVED, THE HOUSE of Deputies concurring, That the 79th General Convention, pursuant to Article X of the Constitution, authorize the ongoing work of liturgical and Prayer Book revision for the future of God's mission through the Episcopal branch of the Jesus movement. And, that it do so upon the core theological work of loving, liberating, life-giving reconciliation and creation care; and be it further

Resolved, that our methodology be one of a dynamic process for discerning common worship, engaging all the baptized, while practicing accountability to The Episcopal Church; and be it further

Resolved, That the 79th General Convention create a Task Force on Liturgical and Prayer Book Revision (TFLPBR), the membership of which will be jointly appointed by the Presiding Bishop and the President of the House of Deputies, and will report to the appropriate legislative committee(s) of the 80th General Convention, ensuring that diverse voices of our church are active participants in this liturgical revision by constituting a group with leaders who represent the expertise, gender, age, theology, regional, and ethnic diversity of the church, to include, 10 laity, 10 priests or deacons, and 10 Bishops; and be it further

Resolved, That this Convention memorialize the 1979 Book of Common Prayer as a Prayer Book of the church preserving the psalter, liturgies, The Lambeth Quadrilateral, Historic Documents, and Trinitarian Formularies ensuring its continued use; and be it further

Resolved, That this church continue to engage the deep Baptismal and Eucharistic theology and practice of the 1979 Prayer Book; and be it further

Resolved, That bishops engage worshiping communities in experimentation and the creation of alternative texts to offer to the wider church, and that each diocese be urged to create a liturgical commission to collect, reflect, teach and share these resources with the TFLPBR; and be it further

Resolved, That the TFLPBR in consultation with the Standing Commission on Structure, Governance, Constitution and Canons is directed to propose to the 80th General Convention revisions to the Constitution and Canons to enable The Episcopal Church to be adaptive in its engagement of future generations of Episcopalians, multiplying, connecting, and disseminating new liturgies for mission, attending to prayer book revision in other provinces of the Anglican Communion; and be it further

Resolved, That liturgical and Prayer Book revision will continue in faithful adherence to the historic rites of the Church Universal as they have been received and interpreted within the Anglican tradition of the 1979 Book of Common Prayer, mindful of our existing ecumenical commitments, while also providing space for, encouraging the submission of, and facilitating the perfection of rites that will arise from the continual movement of the Holy Spirit among us and growing insights of our Church; and be it further

Resolved, That such revision utilize the riches of Holy Scripture and our Church's liturgical, cultural, racial, generational, linguistic, gender, physical ability, class and ethnic diversity in order to share common worship; and be it further

Resolved, That our liturgical revision utilize inclusive and expansive language and imagery for humanity and divinity; and be it further

Resolved, That our liturgical revision shall incorporate and express understanding, appreciation, and care of God's creation; and be it further

Resolved, That our liturgical revision take into consideration the use of emerging technologies which provide access to a broad range of liturgical resources; and be it further

Resolved, That the SCLM create a professional dynamic equivalence translation of The Book of Common Prayer 1979 and the Enriching Our Worship Series in Spanish, French, and Haitian Creole; and that the SCLM diversify the publication formats of new resources, liturgies and rites to include online publishing; and be it further

Resolved, That this church ensure that, at each step of the revision process, all materials be professionally translated into English, Spanish, French, and Haitian Creole, following the principles of dynamic equivalence and that no new rites or liturgical resources be approved by this church until such translations are secured; and be it further

Resolved, That the TFLPBR shall report to the 80th General Convention; and be it further

Resolved, That there being $201,000 in the proposed budget for the translation of liturgical materials, that the Executive Council be encouraged to identify additional funds in the amount of $200,000 to begin this liturgical revision.

Status: Filed

(*Journal of the 79th General Convention* 2018)

1

Changing to Remain the Same

The Evolving Prayer Book Tradition

JEFFREY D. LEE

"THE PRAYER BOOK has to change in order to remain the same," the late Lee Mitchell, one of the great liturgical scholars of the Episcopal Church, was known to say when lecturing on the history of the development of the Book of Common Prayer. In significant ways, that *is* the story of the development of the Book of Common Prayer. Just as every generation in its own context must come to terms with the meaning of scripture or the understanding of God, so too the way we worship, the way we pray together must evolve and adapt in order to be understood in ways that are faithful to the living tradition in which we stand. For the Episcopal Church, The Book of Common Prayer 1979 is simply the most recent example of a long line of versions of the prayer book that embody an ancient pattern of prayer and sacraments that extends to the earliest generation of Christians.

It is arguable that at the heart of the English Reformation was this very question of how to remain faithful to a pattern of worship that would be faithful to and remain in continuity with the faith and practice of the ancient church. In fact, a central question for all the reformers both in England and on the European continent was how to reform what had been received from medieval liturgy in order to recover greater faithfulness to the biblical and early church's understanding and practice of worship and the sacraments. The answer of some Protestant reformers was a radical reshaping of worship in ways that bore little resemblance to the church's worship through the Middle Ages. In England the reforms began somewhat more gently and became more substantial in subsequent revisions of the Book of Common Prayer. From the first modest provisions for prayer and scripture to be delivered in English rather than medieval Latin, successive revisions of the prayer book built on liturgical patterns that were recognizably continuous with those of the medieval church but which began to incorporate more and more elements of reformation theology. This reflected increased attention to what was thought to be premedieval liturgical practice.

The first Book of Common Prayer was authorized for use by Parliament in 1549. Its principal author was the archbishop of Canterbury, Thomas Cranmer. Revisions followed in 1552, 1559, 1604, and finally through to the Book of Common Prayer of 1662, which is still the authorized version in the Church of England. The theological controversies and political complexities of those years all had their effects on these revisions. From the introduction of Reformation influences under Henry VIII and his son Edward VI to a sudden wholesale return to medieval Roman Catholicism under Mary Tudor to the greater stability achieved under Elizabeth I and beyond, monarchical and political concerns and conflicts dominate the story of prayer book revision. An important side note here has to do with political realities in Scotland, where the Reformation took a different course than in England. Under King James I and his son Charles I there were attempts to require Anglicans in Scotland to use the authorized prayer book of the Church of England. Those attempts failed and the result was that the Scottish Church was allowed to produce its own version of the Book of Common Prayer in 1637. The Scottish Prayer Book was more in line with the first prayer book of 1549 and incorporated material that was later to influence the first American version of the Book of Common Prayer (for reasons we will see), influences which are still recognizably present in the Prayer Book 1979.

So it was that after the American Revolution, Anglicans in the new nation were suddenly faced with the existential question of how they were to remain faithful to their identity as Christians whose faith was shaped by a prayer book dominated by royal provision and authorized by Parliamentary decree. How were they to understand themselves as remaining the same while undergoing profound change in a radically new context? No longer a state church, they were now a body of believers free to order their understanding and practice of the Christian faith in ways that were in recognizable continuity with the tradition that formed them, and to do so without reference to Parliament or the crown. Freedom to revise, ongoing liturgical scholarship, and the changing social realities of the new country were to be the driving factors of American prayer book revision in the years to come.

In 1785, a convention of Anglicans from states south of New England met in Philadelphia. The purpose of this first post-revolutionary convention was the pressing question of how to organize the fledgling Episcopal Church. Among several issues before this convention was the place of bishops in the governance of the newly independent church. Bishop Samuel Seabury of Connecticut was the first bishop ordained for the American church, but he had been ordained by bishops in Scotland, where the role of bishops was rather different than that in England as were important aspects of the Scottish Communion Office that had great influence on Seabury. He refused to attend this first convention in part because its proposals did not provide adequately for the role of bishops. Despite the controversies and the absence of representation from the New England states, the 1785 convention did authorize Bishop William White of Pennsylvania, assisted by other bishops, to work on a revision of the Book of Common Prayer. What they produced was a version of the prayer book adopted for use by the Southern states as the proposed prayer book of 1786.

This version was essentially a modification of the 1662 prayer book, but very much influenced by the rationalism and deism of the day. It downplayed core doctrines such as the atonement and the

Holy Trinity. Both the role of bishops and the centrality of the sacraments were likewise less obvious in this book. Naturally, prayers for the monarch were eliminated, but so was the Nicene Creed. The Apostles' Creed remained but the phrase, "He descended into hell" was removed from it. As with almost every revision of the Book of Common Prayer that has followed, it was not popular. Given the variety of conflicting viewpoints and political realties affecting the church at that time, it is difficult to see how any revision could have been received with much general enthusiasm. The Anglican insistence on public adherence to common prayer was in serious doubt, as was the very existence of the church in the United States. A new version of the Book of Common Prayer was sorely needed, and one which could be agreed upon by a majority of both clergy and laity in the newly independent church.

It is remarkable that the first General Convention of the Protestant Episcopal Church, meeting just three years after that first convention of the Southern states, was able in the space of only ten days to produce a revision of the Book of Common Prayer for the church in the United States of America. That the convention of 1789 was able to meet at all, including representation from the New England states, was due in part to the willingness of the Southern states to give up their commitment to the proposed Prayer Book of 1786. There is evidence that the first General Convention was as diverse a gathering as any convention has been since. There were competing opinions about what should be included and what should not. Those who wanted references to the Trinity eliminated and all prayers addressed simply to the Father. Those who wanted to include elements from early church sources and from the Scottish Prayer Book, and those who thought only the slightest adjustments to the Church of England's 1662 book were necessary. In the end, against all the odds, the convention of 1789 produced the first Book of Common Prayer for use in the American church, published in 1790 and titled *The Book of Common Prayer, and Administration of the Sacraments, and Other Rites and Ceremonies of the Church, According to the Use of the Protestant Episcopal Church in the United States of America: together with the Psalter, or Psalms of David.* With the subsequent simplification of the church's name to *the Episcopal Church*, it is the title of every revision of the American Prayer Book down to the Book of Common Prayer 1979.

The 1789 Prayer Book was in use for the next one hundred years. It contains language and liturgical forms that would be recognizable to users of today's prayer book. Importantly, it included a reordering of the eucharistic prayer that can be traced to the 1637 Scottish Prayer Book. Free from the need to adhere strictly to the 1662 Prayer Book of the Church of England, the Scots based this structural rearrangement on scholarly study of ancient West Syrian liturgical models. It included an invocation of the Holy Spirit to "make these gifts for us the Body and Blood of Christ." That invocation of the Spirit over the gifts of bread and wine had been lost in the English Book of 1552 and its recovery has been a permanent one in all authorized versions of the prayer book in the United States since 1789. While individual texts might be familiar to worshipers who pray according to the Book of Common Prayer 1979, other aspects of that first American Prayer Book might not. Overall, ceremonial and architectural settings have changed dramatically since the late eighteenth century — think of the contrast between the simple or even austere setting of a colonial-era church to the elaborate style of a neo-Gothic building from the Victorian era. Musical tastes have evolved and so too has the prayer book's provision for flexibility and choice. The 1789 Book of Common Prayer provided officially for one lengthy, invariable pattern of public prayer on Sundays: Morning Prayer followed by the Litany *and* Holy Communion (although this was often shortened to be the service of Holy Communion only up to and including the sermon). In the nineteenth century, calls for more flexibility and richer ceremonial were to be critical factors in the desire for further prayer book revision.

The nineteenth century witnessed massive and rapid social changes in the United States. From the upheavals precipitating the Civil War and its consequences, to the large scale influx of immigrants into the country, revolutionary industrialization of the economy, the growth of cities and the reality of poverty, slums, and the marginalization of whole communities of persons—all these presented their own challenges to the prayer book's insistence on one, inflexible pattern of worship on the Lord's Day, one that demanded a certain privileged amount of time simply to observe it and a reliance on a literate appreciation of the written word rather than a deeper engagement of the other senses. Gradually it seemed clear to significant leaders in the church that more flexibility and enrichment of the prayer book was necessary in order to meet the pastoral and evangelical needs of the Episcopal Church in a rapidly changing American society.

One name in particular to mention is that of William Augustus Muhlenberg. Born into a distinguished Lutheran family, as a boy he converted to the Episcopal Church and was ordained to the priesthood in 1820. Muhlenberg was a noted educator, the founder of influential church schools, and the rector of the Church of the Holy Communion in New York City. It was there that he initiated practices that would later become in some sense the norm in the Episcopal Church. His motivation was to make the church's worship more appealing and engaging in the lives of the people he served. At the Church of the Holy Communion, he moved the altar to a central position with the pulpit to one side, the worship space was decked with flowers, parts of the service were sung. Muhlenberg allowed the three sections of the required Sunday service to be observed as separate services, and Holy Communion was celebrated weekly. In 1853, in a form called a "Memorial," he called on the General Convention of the Episcopal Church to authorize greater flexibility in the direction of these practices. The Memorial was defeated, but it exercised an ongoing influence on future calls for revisions of the prayer book. In fact, three years later, the House of Bishops agreed that Morning Prayer, the Litany, and Holy Communion could be conducted separately. A genuine revision of the prayer book, however, would not come until 1892. Perhaps Muhlenberg's most important influence has to do with his insistence that the liturgy of the church should have a deep connection with the reality of peoples' lives

In addition to the challenges presented by the changing social and cultural context in which the church pursued its mission, in the nineteenth century a renewed interest in the history of liturgical practice was blossoming. The Oxford Movement arose in the Church of England as a result of controversies about the fundamentally catholic, or universal, character of the church. That is, could Anglicanism genuinely claim continuity with the church of the Middle Ages and earlier? While this movement was not initially concerned primarily with liturgical issues, over time it fostered a greater interest in sacramental theology and the study of liturgy. That interest led to a recovery of ritual in places that was more recognizably "catholic." There were controversies in England, sometimes violent, over matters such as altar candles, vestments, and crosses. In England, these were formal concerns—questions of what was *legally* permissible or not. In the Episcopal Church, although occasionally the cause of conflict, such matters have been left to custom and taste rather than legislated. The adoption of sometimes medieval-looking rituals was thus free to spread quite broadly in the United States.

Through the last half of the nineteenth century, there were ongoing calls in the General Convention for flexibility and enrichment of the prayer book. A priest named William Reed Huntington, an influential member of the House of Deputies, called persistently for revision of the Book of Common Prayer. His leadership was influential in the printing of a version of the prayer book in 1883 known as *The Book Annexed*, which seems to have been intended to demonstrate what a formally revised prayer book might look like. Changes in 1883 and then again in 1886 were approved by the General Convention that went beyond simply the shortening of services, including, for example, the placement of the sermon immediately following the Gospel instead of the Creed, where it had been placed in every version of the prayer book since 1549. The General Convention was demonstrating that it was possible and indeed advisable to revise the prayer book, however cautiously. Against the backdrop of tensions in the church over social issues, as well as theological and liturgical matters, in 1892 the General Convention authorized what was perhaps a predictably modest revision of the Book of Common Prayer. But it was clear that other changes were coming.

The Prayer Book of 1892 was in use just twenty-one years when the official gears were put in motion for further revisions. In 1913 the General Convention formally approved a process for "revising and enriching" the Book of Common Prayer and between then and the General Convention of 1928 that is precisely what happened. At the conventions of 1919 and 1922 large sections of the prayer book were revised for inclusion in the next version. There were again significant differences of opinion on matters to be included or not in the next revision; the 1928 Prayer Book reflected the ongoing evolution of the church's response to a changing world. Significant influences of the day included concerns for issues of social justice, a growing realization of the importance of ecumenical relationships, and (in the shadow of the First World War) the horrific results of global conflicts. Specific changes included the addition of prayer for "The Family of Nations," a collect for Independence Day, the dropping of the word "obey" from the wife's vows in the marriage rite, and provision for the Visitation of the Sick, including the laying on of hands and anointing. Of the more controversial additions were propers for the celebration of the Eucharist at burials and marriages as well as prayers for the departed and the placement of the Lord's Prayer as the conclusion of the Prayer of Consecration. These particular changes were resisted by some out of concern that they were steering the prayer book too far in the direction of Roman Catholic practice, but in fact, the motivation stemmed from then-current liturgical scholarship. Proposals of more obvious similarity to the Roman Rite were rejected, including the *Agnus Dei* (O Lamb of God) and the *Benedictus* (Blessed is he who comes in the name of the Lord) at the conclusion of the *Sanctus* (Holy, Holy, Holy).

In addition to a significant revision of the Book of Common Prayer, the General Convention of 1928 did something else that no previous convention had done in relationship to prayer book revision. It established a Standing Liturgical Commission consisting of eight bishops, eight priests, and eight laypersons for the express purpose of guiding future revisions of the Book of Common Prayer. As recorded in the journal of that convention, the work of the Commission was the "preservation and study, (of) all matters relating to the Book of

Common Prayer, with the idea of developing and conserving for some possible future use the Liturgical experience and scholarship of the Church." This was a frank admission of the need for ongoing evolution of the prayer book in order to remain faithful to its role in a living church.

In the early years of the twentieth century, while the Episcopal Church was engaged in the revision of its Book of Common Prayer, a movement of ecumenical proportions was underway that would eventually transform the worship of all the historic churches. In significant ways, the Reformation and Counter-Reformation both set the stage for the emergence of what came to be called the Liturgical Movement. The reformation period had awakened interest in the origin and roots of Christian worship. Important biblical and historical scholarship was employed by Protestants and Catholics alike to justify their positions. The roots of the contemporary Liturgical Movement can be traced to certain Roman Catholic monastic communities in Europe, and while initially it had little direct impact on either the Church of England or the Episcopal Church, by the 1930s that began to change, and change rapidly.

By the early twentieth century, scholarship had deepened its understanding of source materials describing the fundamental patterns of early church worship and liturgical practice. So much so, in fact, that it was clear that both Protestant and Catholic liturgical practice had become quite removed from that of the early church. The origins of Christian worship are rooted in a fundamental pattern of a community of baptized Christians gathered with its ordained servants to proclaim scripture, to pray, to celebrate and share the eucharistic meal, and then depart to engage in its mission to the needs, hopes, and concerns of the world. All that stood in stark contrast to what had become a clergy-dominated, privatized vision of the liturgy as essentially an act of personal piety. The sweeping liturgical reforms of the Second Vatican Council (1962–1965) were the harbingers of similar reforms soon to be adopted across the Christian world.

In the Episcopal Church, the years between 1928 and 1979 saw an explosion of scholarly work on both the theology and practice of

Christian worship. The names of William Palmer Ladd, who taught at the Berkley Divinity School in New Haven, Connecticut, and his student Massey Shepherd, who taught at the Church Divinity School of the Pacific in California, figure prominently in the spreading appreciation for the insights of the Liturgical Movement. The publication of *The Hymnal 1940* with its rich collection of congregational song also reflected that movement. In 1946, Associated Parishes for Liturgy and Mission was founded: through its publications and conferences, it was to have enormous influence on the development on the Book of Common Prayer 1979.

The General Convention of 1964 called for a plan for a trial usage of a proposed revision of the prayer book. It was a plan for revision unlike any previous one. Involving the work of roughly three hundred consultants and writers who worked with members of the Standing Liturgical Commission, it undertook proposed revisions of every section of the Book of Common Prayer. From 1967 to 1973, the Commission published three books of liturgies for trial usage: *The Liturgy of the Lord's Supper* in 1967, *Services for Trial Use* in 1970, and *Authorized Services* in 1973 (these last two books were known as the "Green Book" and the "Zebra Book" respectively because of the design of their covers). These books for trial liturgies were used throughout the church with responses, critiques, and suggestions collected and considered. One notable outcome of this process of trial use and feedback was the decision to provide both Morning and Evening Prayer and the Holy Eucharist in both contemporary and Elizabethan language (Rite I and Rite II).

The trial changes provoked controversy of course. It was a shock to many members of the church to find suddenly in the pews paperback versions for their use with services containing choices and options to a degree never experienced before. Nevertheless, the trial rites were received thoughtfully for the most part and in 1976 the General Convention approved by overwhelming majorities in both the House of Deputies and the House of Bishops *The Proposed Book of Common Prayer*. Three years later, the General Convention, by nearly unanimous votes, approved the proposed book without any further revisions.

The Book of Common Prayer 1979 continues to shape the life of the Episcopal Church in profound ways that are ongoing. Chief among them are these: the insistence that Holy Baptism is the fundamental sacrament of ministry, that the celebration of the Holy Eucharist is the normative form of worship on the Lord's Day, that participation in the liturgy is the primary source of nourishment for Christian engagement with the world. These convictions endure even as new questions arise about prayer book revision for the twenty-first century and beyond. Indeed, the prayer book changes precisely in order to remain the same.

2

Liturgy for Mission

An Interpretation of Resolution A068

Kevin J. Moroney

Introduction

As delegates to the 79th General Convention of the Episcopal Church prepared to gather in Austin, Texas, in the summer of 2018, participants packed their bags knowing that one of the most significant topics coming before the convention was whether or not to revise the 1979 Book of Common Prayer. At its previous gathering in 2015, the General Convention passed a resolution instructing the Standing Committee on Liturgy and Music (SCLM) to draw up a plan for the comprehensive revision of the prayer book. The SCLM presented two options to the 2018 General Convention:

> Option One . . . envisions a decision by the upcoming General Convention to move into the revision process immediately, the first stage being to gather data, resources, and ideas, and then set up the structure to begin drafting immediately after 2021 General Convention. Option Two . . . envisions a slower pace, while remaining open to Prayer Book revision in the future. Option Two invites the whole church to broaden its familiarity with the 1979 Prayer Book and the history that underlies it, and provides

for time to reflect as a body on the significance of common prayer in our tradition (2018 Blue Book, 194).

The House of Deputies passed Option One, but the House of Bishops replaced it with a much longer and more complex resolution that intends to set the direction of liturgical revision in the Episcopal Church for years to come. The purpose of this essay is to provide an analysis and interpretation of Resolution A068 in order to discern what this new era of liturgical revision may involve.

The resolution itself is a study in Anglican theological method: there is a clear attempt to be comprehensive and inclusive of all traditions and perspectives within the Episcopal Church by providing language that speaks to every group, but in doing so it generates a distinctly Anglican kind of ambiguity that requires interpretive negotiation between the words. In an attempt to clarify the meaning of the resolution, the method employed here will be to reorder the resolution under three major subject headings:

1. The 1979 Prayer Book
2. The Process Going Forward
3. The Envisioned Outcome

In this way all statements related to each topic will be gathered together and interpreted as a whole. When the reordered group is presented, each clause will retain its original number in the resolution, so the reader can see how the reordering was done.

To begin, there are issues addressed in the first resolve that are significant but which are not among the major topics listed above. The first resolve clause reads:

1. . . . That the 79th General Convention . . . authorize the ongoing work of liturgical and Prayer Book revision for the future of God's mission through the Episcopal branch of the Jesus movement. And, that it do so upon the core theological work of loving, liberating, life-giving reconciliation and creation care.

This brief clause asserts that revision is continuous without a prescribed beginning and end, it is for the purpose of Christian mission, and it is set within the thematic framework of our current presiding bishop, Michael Curry, by including language that is taken from his preaching and teaching ministry.

Part I: The 1979 Prayer Book

Our current Book of Common Prayer is cited in four clauses of the Resolution:

4. *Resolved,* That this Convention memorialize the 1979 Book of Common Prayer as a Prayer Book of the church preserving the psalter, liturgies, The Lambeth Quadrilateral, Historic Documents, and Trinitarian Formularies ensuring its continued use; and be it further
5. *Resolved,* That this church continue to engage the deep Baptismal and Eucharistic theology and practice of the 1979 Prayer Book; and be it further
8. *Resolved,* That liturgical and Prayer Book revision will continue in faithful adherence to the historic rites of the Church Universal as they have been received and interpreted within the Anglican tradition of 1979 Book of Common Prayer, mindful of our existing ecumenical commitments, while also providing space for, encouraging the submission of, and facilitating the perfection of rites that will arise from the continual movement of the Holy Spirit among us and growing insights of our Church; and be it further
13. *Resolved,* That the SCLM create a professional dynamic equivalence translation of The Book of Common Prayer 1979 and the Enriching Our Worship Series in Spanish, French, and Haitian Creole; and that the SCLM diversify the publication formats of new resources, liturgies, and rites to include online publishing.

These clauses appear to be an attempt to strike some balance regarding the status of our current prayer book. On the one hand it is memorialized (without any specific clarification of exactly what that means), particular parts are to be preserved, its continued use is ensured, and its baptismal and eucharistic theology is to be engaged further. Additionally, clause 13 calls for dynamic equivalence translations of the 1979 Prayer Book into all official languages of the Episcopal Church, which suggests that it will be available in its current form for the foreseeable future. These assertions would all be very welcome by those who, for various reasons, do not want to alter our current book or have any new book supersede it.

On the other hand, 1979 Prayer Book clause 8 refers to prayer book revision as something that is a part of this new era, and it further describes the "perfection of rites" that is stated within the context of the 1979 Prayer Book, which can only mean that revision work is envisioned for the current book. These assertions would be welcomed by those who feel that the current prayer book needs to be revised.

Some have proposed that memorializing the '79 book could lead us into a practice like that of the Church of England, where the prayer book is perpetual but where alternative rites abound. While that is true for England, it is due to complications related to being the church established by law. The Church of England attempted to pass revised prayer books through Parliament in 1927 and 1928 but, after both failed for what were largely political reasons, in time they passed legislation to allow alternative rites. In other words, it's the system they have created to adapt to their unique circumstances, rather than the system they might want. We could adopt such a system, but that does not appear to be the intention of the resolution, given the number of references to prayer book revision.

Another option could be to have a revised prayer book, but keep the rites of the '79 book available. When the Church of Ireland revised its prayer book in 2004, the Coverdale Psalter from the 1926 Prayer Book continued to be available in digital form. There is nothing stopping us from keeping the 1979 Prayer Book available even with a newly revised prayer book. The principle that the Church of Ireland followed was to force change as little as possible, but to introduce enrichment for those who desired it. We could adopt a version of that principle here in the Episcopal Church.

Whichever direction is ultimately chosen, the parts of the resolution that relate to the 1979 Prayer Book indicate that revision work will be done and the current rites will remain in use. What is not yet known is the duration of this arrangement.

Part II: The Process Going Forward

2. *Resolved,* that our methodology be one of a dynamic process for discerning common worship, engaging all the baptized, while practicing accountability to The Episcopal Church; and be it further
3. *Resolved,* That the 79th General Convention create a Task Force on Liturgical and Prayer Book Revision (TFLPBR), the membership of which will be jointly appointed by the Presiding Bishop and the President of the House of Deputies, and will report to the appropriate legislative committee(s) of the 80th General Convention, ensuring that diverse voices of our church are active participants in this liturgical revision by constituting a group with leaders who represent the expertise, gender, age, theology, regional, and ethnic diversity of the church, to include, 10 laity, 10 priests or deacons, and 10 Bishops; and be it further
6. *Resolved,* That bishops engage worshiping communities in experimentation and the creation of alternative texts to offer to the wider church, and that each diocese be urged to create a liturgical commission to collect, reflect, teach and share these resources with the TFLPBR; and be it further
7. *Resolved,* That the TFLPBR in consultation with the Standing Commission on Structure, Governance, Constitution and Canons is directed to propose to the 80th General Convention revisions to the Constitution and Canons to enable The Episcopal Church to be adaptive in its engagement of future generations of Episcopalians, multiplying, connecting, and disseminating new liturgies for mission, attending to prayer book revision in other provinces of the Anglican Communion . . .

From the minute this resolution was passed, attention was immediately directed toward the creation of the task force described in clause 3 as the central decision of the document. The General Convention created a thirty-member task force, including a balance from the orders of ministry, and attempting to include a wide array of demographic diversity in the Episcopal Church. This is certainly an important decision, and it is understandable that, as the group charged with carrying out the work of the resolution, this task force was going to get a lot of attention. However, in clause 2 there is a statement that arguably carries greater historical and theological significance, but has gone largely unmentioned. In that clause we read of "a dynamic process for discerning common worship, engaging all the baptized. . . ." Language about engaging all the baptized is employed so often today that it can be read as religious jargon, but in the context of liturgical revision it is quite revolutionary. Throughout Christian history, liturgical revision has been done by liturgical specialists and church officials. The Liturgical Movement of the second half of the twentieth century placed a new and intentional emphasis on the full, conscious, and active participation of all the people in the liturgy, but the revisions that came out during that era were still by and large the work of specialists and officials. Many revisions of that era did go to considerable lengths to receive feedback from the laity, and the 1979 Prayer Book was preceded by trial liturgies that went out to parishes and generated feedback. It was more inclusive of nonspecialists than that of previous efforts at revision, but A068 goes notably further by calling all the baptized to participate at the level of liturgical creation. This makes our new era of revision one that is intended to be "bottom up" or "baptized up" for the first time.

Bishops are to work directly with parishes on liturgical experimentation and creation. This goes well beyond what the prayer book or canons currently allow bishops to authorize, and sends us into an era of liturgical trial and error that will be liberation to some and alarming to others. In order for this process to be effective, each bishop must be actively encouraging and overseeing creative experimentation, have full knowledge of what is actually being done, and set reasonable limits on what is authorized locally. Bishops are also charged to make sure that their diocese has a liturgical commission that can receive the creative liturgies being used, assess them, and share these resources with the task force that was created in clause 3.

Just as bishops interface with parishes and liturgical commissions, the task force interfaces between liturgical commissions and the General Convention. The task force first met on November 11–13, 2018, and released a report at the end of that meeting:

> The Task Force spent considerable time studying their mandate as set forth in General Convention Resolution A-068. Alongside the continuing use of the Book of Common Prayer 1979, it seems clear that the church also desires to expand the breadth of its liturgical prayer to include richer biblical and theological language and new rites that are needed for particular missional contexts, while continuing our historic commitment to the biblical roots of our public prayer and to traditional Anglican liturgical and sacramental formularies.
>
> The Task Force has divided its work into four working groups. The groups will collect and evaluate various experimental rites already in use in the church, determine the best way to screen and distribute the rites for further consultation, determine appropriate recommendations for changes to the Constitution and Canons of the church to invigorate liturgical development, and consider continuing enrichment of our current liturgical materials.
>
> In the course of the triennium, the Task Force will provide multiple ways to receive input from across the church, listen to many voices, and regularly update the church on the progress of its work.

One mandate given to the task force is to work with the Standing Commission on Structure, Governance, Constitution and Canons to create a more streamlined process for approving new rites. The current canons regarding liturgical authorization are fairly restrictive. Rites for trial use and alterations to the lectionary can be passed by vote of one convention, but anything relating to alterations to the Book of Common Prayer requires approval by two successive General Conventions (*Constitutions and Canons* 2018, 12–13). So when the resolution calls for a change to the canons that would enable us to be more "adaptive," it is clear that the intention is for a faster process of authorization.

At this past General Convention, a resolution was passed that maintains the two convention requirement for alterations to the Prayer Book, but would change the canon to allow passage by one convention for "alternative and additional liturgies to supplement those provided in the Book of Common Prayer" (General Convention Website, Resolutions). If this resolution is passed again in 2021, the canon will be changed and a faster process for alternative rites will be accomplished.

What may be emerging at this stage of analysis is a four-track system:

1. The preservation and continued use of the 1979 Prayer Book
2. Diocesan bishops will work with parishes and liturgical commissions to create and authorize alternative liturgies within each diocese, and forward their best fruit to the task force or other body subsequently authorized by the General Convention
3. A slower track for the revision of the 1979 Prayer Book, maintaining a two convention approval process
4. A one convention approval process for alternative liturgies that are not intended for the prayer book.

This would provide freedom for all the baptized to create and experiment under Episcopal authority. It would also provide new legislation that would enable Episcopalians to be "more adaptive" in approving new, alternative liturgies more quickly. And it would ensure the theological and textual stability of the 1979 Prayer Book both by the assurance of its continued availability for use and the commitment that it will be the basis of any future prayer book revision.

Part III: The Envisioned Outcome

9. *Resolved,* That such revision utilize the riches of Holy Scripture and our Church's liturgical, cultural, racial, generational, linguistic, gender, physical ability, class and ethnic diversity in order to share common worship; and be it further
10. *Resolved,* That our liturgical revision utilize inclusive and expansive language and imagery for humanity and divinity; and be it further

11. *Resolved*, That our liturgical revision shall incorporate and express understanding, appreciation, and care of God's creation; and be it further
12. *Resolved*, That our liturgical revision take into consideration the use of emerging technologies which provide access to a broad range of liturgical resources; and be it further
14. *Resolved*, That this church ensure that, at each step of the revision process, all materials be professionally translated into English, Spanish, French, and Haitian Creole, following the principles of dynamic equivalence and that no new rites or liturgical resources be approved by this church until such translations are secured; and be it further
15. *Resolved*, That the TFLPBR shall report to the 80th General Convention . . .

One of the truths and challenges for Anglicans when it comes to any discussion of liturgy is our tendency to default to the Book of Common Prayer. And the prayer book has been referenced seven times in Resolution A068. This makes it all the more striking that, in this third and final area of concern, the prayer book is not mentioned once. The preferred language here is that of "liturgical revision," which reflects an attempt of the total resolution to include but not be limited to revision of the Book of Common Prayer. These clauses of the resolution list the areas of concern that should be applied to all revision work, and for those who work in the field of liturgy they are not new issues: mindfulness of every demographic, inclusive and expansive language for God and people, a theology of creation, different media platforms, and dynamic equivalence translations into all official languages of the Episcopal Church. However, this is also where the work could become controversial.

When the resolution describes utilizing the richness found in cultural, racial, and ethnic diversity, we have arrived at the doorstep of a broader issue that has been very important in liturgical theology over the last fifty years, that of inculturation: affirming and utilizing different forms of art, music, language, and expression. The Episcopal Church has made some efforts in this area, such as a Spanish translation of the

1979 Prayer Book and the African American hymnal *Lift Every Voice and Sing II*, but this clause is an acknowledgement that inculturation is a concern that needs to find expression in all our revision work. For example, one reason the resolution refers to "dynamic equivalence translations" is because the prayer book in Spanish is generally recognized as an inadequate literal translation that does not include the idiomatic phrases that are used by actual Spanish speakers.

Inclusive and expansive language begins with the premise that male forms of language do not represent all people and does not represent the fullness of God. Therefore, a commitment is made in the resolution to use gender neutral terms for people and a wider range of images for God in our revision work. For some, attention to inclusive and expansive language in the prayer book is long overdue. For others, images for God that expand beyond the language of our current prayer book raises concerns about what sources will be used for that language, and how any changes in our language about God will affect our doctrine of the Trinity and each person of the Trinity.

Regarding creation theology, the 1979 Prayer Book does show signs of increased concern about what we now call creation care, but Eucharistic Prayers C and D both refer to humanity as rulers of creation, and our catechism begins with "Human Nature" when it might better begin with a section on creation itself, providing a balanced articulation between humanity's place within, responsibility for, and influence upon creation.

One question the task force will have to wrestle with is the extent to which these linguistic and theological principles are applied equally throughout all rites, and the path forward may be determined by how long the 1979 Prayer Book is authorized for use. If it will be available perpetually, then a more thorough revision of those rites should not be controversial to those who have access to our current rites. However, if the 1979 rites will only be available until a full revision is approved, we will then need to decide whether language changes to those rites will be made to a lesser extent so that members who prefer those liturgies as they are now will not feel forced into a change they do not desire. A consistent policy will need to be developed and implemented.

The provision for the use of emerging technologies made in clause 12 may provide a helpful path forward. Digital publication removes the limits that are imposed when the media platform is a book; with digital material there would be no limit to how much liturgical material could be authorized and produced. A decision may be made regarding whether digital material would only be approved at the one convention level or, if some digital material shares the same doctrinal and liturgical consensus as the Book of Common Prayer, would that digital material be authorized at the two-convention level? There is a balance to be found between the richness found in a diversity of liturgies and the value placed on having liturgies for the entire Episcopal Church. General Convention will ultimately have to decide where the balance point is.

The provision made in clause 15 that all approved liturgical material be translated into all of the official languages of the Episcopal Church, and that no new liturgies be approved until "such translations are secured," may serve to ensure that this process will not move too quickly. While what it means to secure a translation remains ambiguous, it does put a road block on what would otherwise be the easier process of rapidly approving new English language liturgies with a promise of future translations that may or may not ever happen. Whatever it is determined to mean, the translations of the new liturgies must be secured before new liturgies can be approved. No translations, no new liturgies!

Clause 15 of the resolution simply states that the task force will report to the next General Convention in 2021, and the resolution ends with clause 16 noting that the national budget already has $201,000 for translation of liturgical materials, and Executive Council is encouraged to provide $200,000 to begin the work.

Conclusion

Resolution A068 describes how we will begin this new era of liturgical revision, but in places it can appear unclear or even contradictory. What is the status of the 1979 Prayer Book? We will memorialize it and we will revise it. How will we produce revisions and new liturgies? We will have widespread creative freedom and we will be under diocesan and national authority. How will new liturgies be approved? We will have a local process and we will have a national process. Essentially, the resolution was written to include all perspectives without excluding any possibilities, but that will require the General Convention to make important decisions as we go through this process.

The key to success will be the extent to which those who are identified in the resolution fully take on their roles. Will the baptized answer the call? Will bishops actively work with both parishes and liturgical commissions? Will the task force be able to lead and oversee such a multilayered church-wide program? The answers to these questions will be uneven, but the Episcopal Church is to be commended for choosing to expand its vision rather than contract it. We will move forward more slowly than some, and more rapidly than others, would prefer. But we are moving forward and are doing so for the purpose of resourcing the entire Episcopal Church with worship materials that will assist our people in carrying out our mission.

Questions for Discussion

1. What does it mean to "memorialize" the 1979 Prayer Book?
2. In what ways can "all the baptized" be engaged in this era of liturgical revision?
3. What kind of creative liturgies are needed in the Episcopal Church today?
4. Do you agree that inclusive language for God and people is important and, if so, why?
5. How would you implement a more ecological theology into the prayer book?

3

Common Prayer, a Strong Thread

Kathryn A. Rickert

"[W]hen Anglicanism is at its best its liturgy, its poetry, its music and its life
can create a world of wonder in which it is very easy to fall in love with God."
—Urban T. Holmes III, *What Is Anglicanism?*

"The people of this congregation (I mean ye Church's real Friends, ye communicants) universally disapprove of ye new Book . . ."
—Thomas Clagget, first Bishop of Maryland, reporting on the reception of the Proposed Prayer Book of 1786 (Sydnor 1997, 58.)

IN RESPONSE TO General Convention Resolution A-068 of 2018, we enter once again a process of reflection and discernment to "ensur[e] that [the] diverse voices of our church are active participants in this liturgical revision" in order to extend the reach of common prayer to *all* of the baptized. We need to consider carefully how it is that common prayer nurtures the lives of those who follow Jesus in this way.

Each version of the Book of Common Prayer from 1549 through the present is woven through with a strong thread of five qualities: sufficiency, spaciousness, humility, usefulness, and timeliness. These qualities appear in each era, albeit not in the same ways or for the same reasons. The fundamental heart of common prayer is that God's people pray together in public in language and ways that they can use, given their time and place. Each change of time and place has called for and come up with revisions and additions. As in the past, so now, some of those revisions and additions are transformations of earlier understandings of the Divine-human relationship and what it means to follow Jesus as Episcopalians: the abolition of slavery, recognition of the human agency and dignity of women and Indigenous peoples, democracy rather than empire, and our sacred responsibility to care for creation.

The fabric of common prayer draws together for public prayer "all sorts and conditions" of God's people, both those who follow Jesus, and others as well. "All sorts and conditions" includes many other people of faith or no faith who have other connections to this tradition through weddings, funerals, film, literature, music, architecture, and the strong appeal of liturgical worship to less liturgical Christians.

As we discern and prepare to revise and update the Book of Common Prayer, it is important to consider how these five qualities fit our time and place, and those to come. Prayer Book revision has never been easy; there are always differences and divisions. Each edition of the Book of Common Prayer made a strong yet imperfect effort to encourage "all sorts and conditions" of God's people to pray together in public, given the needs and constraints of their time and place.

We might think that common prayer has sustained public prayer as well as it has primarily because of the specific words and gestures called for on the pages of Book of Common Prayer. Yet, if we look further, we find something more complex behind the pages. What appears on the pages or screens is the fruit of faithful lives that gave birth to the words and gestures. For when those whose lives are deeply marked by common prayer describe their experiences, it is as though the disparate, contesting parts of their lives are gently, yet respectfully connected by a strong thread to a greater whole. This thread passes through diverse events high and low, joys, sorrow, suffering, failure, success, desires, boredom, wondering, disappointments, and fears "known and unknown," from before birth and on through the final breath and rest in the Holy One. At times the thread is invisible, yet still present. It may be any color or texture needed in order to suit those lives, in that context. When embodied, they may serve to form God's people into a faithful body, followers of Jesus. Such prayer proclaims with both words and actions the reconciling justice and love of Jesus. It allows us to mourn our losses, to repent of our sins, to cry out to God from our distress, and to pray for the well-being of others and the whole creation. The voice of common prayer conveys "respect for the dignity of every human being" that seeks to "serve Christ in all persons," and to care for creation. It honors differences while supporting connection, without seeking sameness that denies difference.

The thread of common prayer gathers together what we need to participate in the reconciliation of "all sorts and conditions," not by holding anyone down so that differences are glossed over, or ignored, but rather by acknowledging and honoring the glorious, rich diversity of God's people. This pattern is found not so much in specific language, as it is the qualities of faithful lives that gave life to and nurtured this language over nearly five hundred years. Given the needs and constraints of our time and place, this thread will lead to new words, gestures, and faithful lives marked by sufficiency, spaciousness, humility, usefulness, and timeliness.

1. **Sufficiency**—means enough, but not all, knowledge, faith, and wisdom to make way for the wonder, mystery, and grace of God alongside human variation and frailty.
2. **Spaciousness**—means enough room to move around within the realms of faith so as to be adapted to many cultures and contexts by using "may," "or," and alternatives.
3. **Humility**—means that however great our knowledge and our love of God may be, they are also incomplete and imperfect.

4. **Usefulness**—means that common prayer fulfills the needs and constraints upon public worship of the time and places of the people who use it, on their terms.
5. **Timeliness** (both ancient and modern)—means that the past is brought into conversation with the present to create new life for the future. The measure to which these five qualities are present in the Book of Common Prayer of the future will contribute mightily to public worship for all "sorts and conditions."

These five qualities may help us to understand *how* it is that common prayer connects God to us, to each other, and to creation. It may serve to guide the "Episcopal branch of the Jesus movement" for "a dynamic process for discerning common worship" by "all the baptized" in the work of "loving, liberating, life-giving reconciliation, and creation care."(A068 paragraph 1) Following the wisdom of the prophetic tradition, we consider here the past of common prayer in order to discern what the present calls us to do for the future of the Episcopal Church.

1. Sufficiency

Almighty God, to you all hearts are open,
all desires known, and from you no secrets are hid:

(BCP, 355)

Sufficiency means enough, but not all, knowledge, faith, and wisdom to make way for the wonder, mystery, and grace of God alongside of human variation and frailty.

"Sufficiency" is found in the Collect for Purity with which many eucharistic celebrations begin. In few words, and fewer qualifiers as to place, kind, or time, this collect declares—just enough to gather us together, yet not so much as to pry into the details of these hearts, desires, or secrets in ways that set apart. Sufficiency says just enough to lead to things we cannot measure—love, fear, evil, compassion, gratitude, anger, joy, wisdom, longing, patience, and reconciliation. It leaves room for what we do not know how to say.

However different from each other we may be, we are also alike. We all experience these things we cannot measure. All life, human and nonhuman, shares *some* experience of birth, living, and dying. Yet, the variations within God-created human and nonhuman birth, life, and death/joys and sorrows are *unlimited*. We all have hearts, desires, and secrets; the details vary.

By "sufficiency" common prayer draws God's people together enough to pray in public, not because we are exactly alike or pray in exactly the same ways, but because we share these unmeasured things at our core.

Something like "sufficiency" appears in the Old Testament directions for building the dwelling in which God traveled with Israel in the wilderness (see Exod. 25:10, 16). The purpose of these detailed "instructions" is not to serve as a blueprint for building construction, but rather, to convey a message about the unmeasurable and awesome presence of the portable God with Israel on the wilderness journey (Fox 1995, 394). It is just enough information to convey the value and honor attached to a place of worship, but not enough to actually build one. Through "sufficiency," common prayer helps gather people together around the important, worthy, holy, and shared.

2. Spaciousness

Keep watch, dear Lord, with those who work, or watch, or weep this night, and give your angels charge over those who sleep. Tend the sick, Lord Christ; give rest to the weary, bless the dying, soothe the suffering, pity the afflicted, shield the joyous; and all for your love's sake. Amen.

(BCP, 124)

Spaciousness means there is room to move around throughout the realms of faith by means of "may," "or," (as in the above) and choices from among alternatives.

A comprehensive rather than exhaustive approach to the many "sorts and conditions" of God's people creates space for a full array of feelings, ecstasy to despair, and all in-between. Spaciousness helps us to grapple as awkwardly as necessary with the actual joys and sorrows of life and ministry according to our particular context and experience.

If one observes carefully what people are actually saying and doing in worship, one will notice interesting variations in speech and gestures by laity and clergy alike. Official and unofficial, intentional and accidental additions, omissions, and local options made in worship include private revisions of the liturgy through gender changes, names or issues added or omitted, silence, increased intensity, etc. Variations in movement and gesture include: crossing oneself, or not; solemn bows at the aisle, or not; genuflection; hands folded, or not; arms raised; hands held out from the waist; heads bowed; eyes open/closed; vestments or street clothing; kneeling; standing; sitting; the particular sequence of parts of the liturgy (i.e., announcements, etc.). Through spaciousness created by these variations, official and those people come up with on their own, no two Episcopal liturgies using the Book of Common Prayer are *exactly* alike in all things. Common prayer makes praying-together-while-different possible by making room for the particular.

Because some congregations use only a few pages of the Book of Common Prayer, or paper copies of the liturgies, many are unfamiliar with other parts of the Book of Common Prayer. It is easy to think that what we are doing in this congregation is exactly what the directions call for, and thus, the same as that of every other congregation using the Book of Common Prayer. By the spaciousness of common prayer, these variations are welcome and even necessary for the worship by all sorts and conditions. Such variations make room for difference, so that many can come together in common prayer. There is room for each to be who we are, without demanding that someone else pretend to be who he or she is not.

3. Humility

> *We limit not the truth of God*
> *to our poor reach of mind,*
> *to notions of our day and sect . . .*

[for God] has yet more light and truth
to break forth from [the] word.
  Hymnal 1982, #629 Words: George Rawson, 1807–1889

Where it is corrupt, purify it;
where it is in error, direct it;
where in anything it is amiss, reform it.
  (Prayer for the Church, BCP, 816)

Humility means that however great our knowledge and our love of God may be, they are also incomplete and imperfect.

Common prayer is *not* the only way to live a Christian spiritual and ethical life. Neither is it perfect. This surely is one of the strongest aspects of the thread; a sharp, never-to-be-lost awareness of the incompleteness of our understanding of and faithfulness to God, each other, and creation. Rather, this still unfolding way of following Jesus has been life-giving, inspiring, liberating, and spiritually formative in the lives of millions of people for nearly five hundred years. Yes, it is primarily British and Western in its origins; nevertheless, common prayer has made its way to many nations and world cultures. We continue to struggle to be open and learn from each other. Each of these cultures contributes something to the larger common prayer. Our understandings today of "all sorts and conditions" in church and society have drastically changed since the Book of Common Prayer 1549. Alongside of this thread is another thread that painfully laments and seeks to repent of the "manifold sins" of failure "to strive for justice and peace among *all* people."

Each edition of the Book of Common Prayer has been met with a sense that it is not yet complete, finished, perfect, and that further changes would be necessary in the future. Now, part of the task of Book of Common Prayer expansion/revision bids us to appreciate more fully the impact of any one era's experiences on *their* understanding of common prayer. And then, go on to consider that for ourselves and for those who come after us. We only participate in our relationship with God and others through the particularities of our own experiences. With humility we can own and honor our experience, while also granting that same honor to those who have different experiences and understandings of God.

4. Usefulness

> *XXIV. Of Speaking in the Congregation in such a Tongue as the people understandeth. It is a thing plainly repugnant to the Word of God, and the custom of the Primitive Church, to have public Prayer in the Church, or to minister the Sacraments, in a tongue not understanded of the people.*
>
> (Articles of Religion, BCP, 872)

Usefulness means that common prayer fulfills the needs and constraints upon public worship of the time and places of the people who use it, on their terms.

The next generation of resources for common prayer is coming to be for the same fundamental reasons that each of the other versions did, in order to be *useful* to the people of God, in this *time* and place, and on *their* terms. A Book of Common Prayer bound in red or black leather, with gold edges and embossed in gold with one's name is a precious and spiritually life-giving book for some Episcopalians. While others know that they can find much, but not all, of that—the dedication page and the gold embossing on the cover—in their phones, or on their computers. Both versions of common prayer serve as rich food for spiritual, ethical lives.

Many whose lives are marked by the strong thread of common prayer speak of a "particular fit" to their lives. Over time the words and gestures become intimately woven into their lives. "Fit" is also used by those who "discover" the Episcopal Church as adults. Common prayer resonates with the contours of their lives, of their souls, while at the same time honoring the distinctions in other lives. By overtly seeking to bring together "all sorts and conditions," common prayer gathers together in ways that our society increasingly does not.

When someone struggles with prayer language, hymns, or gestures, etc., it is often described by "that does not fit me." "That is not my experience of God, or of myself." Thus, our next versions of Book of Common Prayer will continue to seek to be fitting to more "sorts and conditions" of God's people. This measure of "usefulness" is not visible only in its appeal to Episcopalians, but also to millions who know it only from funerals, weddings, and movies. Common prayer is religious language that also manages to make room for those who do not follow Jesus in ways that much religious language does not.

The earliest versions of Book of Common Prayer were written in English rather than Latin for the same reasons that future versions of the Book of Common Prayer and alternative texts will be found in dynamic translations of other languages such as Spanish, French, Hawaiian, Lakota, Navajo, Ojibwa, etc. and in different styles and formats that are understandable to the people who use them.

5. Timeliness (Both Ancient and Modern)

We receive you into the household of God. Confess the faith of Christ crucified, proclaim his resurrection, and share with us in his eternal priesthood. (BCP, 308)

Christ has died, Christ is risen, Christ will come again. (BCP, 363)

Timeliness insists that the past not be forgotten, but rather sifted through and brought into conversation with the present in order to receive new life in these contexts for the future.

The sacred past is old, not stale; venerable, not stuck, preserved, but not frozen. It continues to give life for the future to those who pay attention to it. Like a sacred time machine, common prayer places us simultaneously within the communion of saints, fully present in the here and now, and into the coming reign of God. In some ways, it is both ancient and modern, and postmodern all at once. Through the language and gestures of common prayer, our attention and presence are not isolated in the present. By weaving traditional "sacred" language together with the particularities of *this* time and place—the names of actual people, places, and events—common prayer accomplishes a reconciling connection between different eras that is otherwise unlikely. The most timely thing worship can do is to help make the God of history and experience present in today's context, so that God's people might gather to pray, to give thanks, to become more fully formed in the birth, life, death, and resurrection of Jesus, the Christ for the world today, and in the future.

What Do We Mean by "Common Prayer, and Common"?

O God, the creator and preserver of all mankind,
we humbly beseech thee for all sorts and conditions of men;
that thou wouldest be pleased to make thy ways known unto them,
thy saving health unto all nations. . . . (BCP, 814)

Nobody was satisfied with the 1549 Prayer Book.
(All prayer books seem to suffer this fate!) (Lee 1999, 51)

As we prepare for additional resources for public prayer that reflects the context of those to come, it may help to reconsider our understanding of the word "common." The "common" in common prayer does not mean low or imply a unity that resists diversity. From the beginning of this tradition, the connective powers of this strong thread have intentionally sought (not always successfully) to make it possible for people who are *very* different from each other and even *deeply* divided, to somehow nevertheless manage to pray together in public. This is the genius of common prayer. Within the dangerously violent upheavals of the Reformation, differences of social class, geography, historical and political connections as well opposing views on Christian theology and worship were brought together awkwardly at first, very imperfectly, and with considerable risk of failure: common prayer made public worship possible.

Common prayer never did and never will mean that we who pray together are all alike and agree with each other in most things. Rather, through this strong thread of sufficiency, spaciousness, humility, usefulness, and timeliness, common prayer has managed to convey this motley crew of divided, excluded, and excluding peoples of

God together in many places long enough for us to acknowledge the wonders of grace, the pains of life, to cry out in distress, to seek God's presence, and to give thanks before heading out on our distinct ways to be God's people in the world. The future of common prayer depends upon a radical extension of the strong thread of sufficiency, spaciousness, humility, usefulness, and timeliness so that public worship continues to be possible for "all sorts and conditions" of God's people.

We have this strong thread not because of the words on the pages of Book of Common Prayer, but rather because of centuries of faithful lives, those who have fallen in love with God and followed Jesus in this way. This thread is the fruit of those lives manifest in common prayer, and as such, food and formation for our lives of faith. So will be the future of the Book of Common Prayer. However well thought out, however elegant and inspiring the additions and revisions to Book of Common Prayer may be, the future strength of this thread depends upon how we live the words we pray.

Questions for Discussion

1. How does having enough but not all knowledge, faith, or wisdom make way for the wonder and mystery of God in worship? (See the Collect for Purity, BCP, 355.)
2. Where do you find options for choice from among alternatives for worship in Evening Prayer II, the use of "may," "or," "and"? What do these choices contribute to these prayers? (See BCP, 115–26.)
3. How does the Book of Common Prayer invite and contribute to worship that is marked by humility? (See the Prayer for the Church, BCP, 816.)
4. In what ways does common prayer include or exclude you? Include or exclude others whose lives differ greatly from yours?
5. How do the past and the future of the Christian tradition matter for your faith life now in the present? How does the past contribute to our worship today? What will make common prayer useful to future generations?

4

The Episcopal Church

So Much More than a National Church

SYLVIA SWEENEY

RESOLUTION 9 OF A068 states, "*Resolved,* That such revision utilize the riches of Holy Scripture and our Church's liturgical, cultural, racial, generational, linguistic, gender, physical ability, class and ethnic diversity in order to share common worship." This resolution asks that we not only make room within our worship life for Americans who speak other languages and have other cultural and ethnic identities, it also asks that the church acknowledge the breadth of histories and cultures beyond the United States that worship from our prayer book and have their theologies, ecclesiology, and worldviews shaped by it. The resolution invites us into a shared worship life that moves beyond culturally dominant English-speaking American expectations of what Episcopalians look like and sound like to a new vision of the church that is conscious of and appreciative of our diversity and differences. This intentionality can offer twenty-first-century Episcopalians a fresh vision for what common worship can be in this new millennium. The implication is that common worship is not uniform worship. Quite the contrary, common worship allows us to find the resources that permit diverse peoples to hold a common faith and love of Christ within the context of their own varied personal and cultural identities. Learning from one another in celebration of our differences allows us to hold more in common, not less.

Misssiologist Lamin Sanneh asserts that one of the central hallmarks of the Christian faith has been its multilingual, multicultural character from its inception. While other religious traditions may require learning a sacred language in order to engage in faith practices, Christianity has grown up in the vernacular. Christian sacred texts have existed in multiple languages since our scriptures and liturgies were first spoken and written. One need only read the New Testament to understand that the Christian Church saw itself as multilingual and multicultural from its very beginnings. The story of Pentecost and the birth of the Church is a story of a faith proclamation that could resonate across cultural boundaries: a universal message that held a potency of meaning that allowed it to change and grow and thrive as it touched the cultures of those it came in contact with. Something in the core message of Christianity allowed it to continue to bless and save human beings who did not come from the religious, cultural, or philosophical world of first-century Galilean Judaism. Sanneh asserts that as Christians encountered the world, they allowed the world to hear and receive and translate the Good News of Jesus Christ.

In church-wide discourse it is still common to hear the Episcopal Church described as the national church. Actually, the Episcopal Church is made up of dioceses that stretch across sixteen nations and four continents, with Episcopalians living in Europe, in Asia and the Pacific Islands, in Central America, and in North America and the Caribbean. The most populated diocese of our church is the Diocese of Haiti with over 83,000 members and over one hundred churches. Episcopalians worship in Creole, French, German, Flemish, Spanish, Italian, Tagalong, Igorot, Taiwanese, Mandarin, Cantonese, Korean, Vietnamese, Navajo, Lakota, and English, along with other indigenous languages. This chapter will explore the history of the development of Episcopal dioceses outside the geographic and political boundaries of the United States and discuss the ways in which our Episcopal global identity experience in an increasingly globalized context must help shape the development of our next prayer book.

Historian and missiologist Ian Douglas asserts that the concept of a national church is a fairly recent development in the history of the Episcopal Church. The office of the presiding bishop was not founded until 1919 and signaled a new era in the church's life in which the Episcopal Church came to see itself as having a national identity within a larger global context. As the United States became a global power on the world stage, American Episcopalians began to see their church as an important institution in promoting Anglicanism in the world. Remembering that the Episcopal Church is a young church, having been formed as its own jurisdiction following the Revolutionary War in the United States, much of the history of the Episcopal Church has grown out of the development of the church first during the westward expansion of the Episcopal Church in the United States and then more recently during the period of missionary efforts undertaken by the Episcopal Church as it became an influential member of the Anglican Communion. There are currently 110 Episcopal dioceses in the United States, Colombia, Cuba, the Dominican Republic, Ecuador, Haiti, Honduras, Puerto Rico, Taiwan, Micronesia, Venezuela, and the Virgin Islands. The Convocation of Episcopal Churches in Europe and the Navajoland Area Mission are jurisdictions similar to a diocese. Liturgical renewal offers Episcopalians the opportunity to celebrate this deeply diverse and culturally and spiritually rich identity.

Much of the history of the expansion of the Episcopal Church beyond the boundaries of the United States is directly related to missionary efforts that the church engaged in from the late nineteenth century forward as Episcopalians began to look for new lands to evangelize. During the late twentieth century, several dioceses that were formerly part of the Episcopal Church as missionary dioceses left the Episcopal Church and became their own autonomous provinces in the Anglican Communion. The former Diocese of Mexico founded in 1879 became the Province of Mexico in 1995. In 1998 the Province of Central America was formed from five Central American dioceses. Even earlier the Diocese of Brazil became its own province in 1965.

The principles that played a key role in this move to autonomy for some missionary dioceses was a philosophical shift in understandings of mission work. Early missionary efforts grew from an understanding of mission work as focused on sharing the economic, cultural, and spiritual wealth of American Episcopalians with those outside the United States with fewer economic resources. Much of the impetus for these early missionary efforts was a desire to bring the social gospel to poorer nations, to offer aid by building hospitals, schools, and churches. In this era, there were many women missionaries founding schools and hospitals while clergy men concentrated most of their efforts on building churches and recruiting worshippers. This age of missionary work reached its zenith at the same time that the United States' political, economic, and cultural influences in the world were sharply rising.

Ian Douglas identifies the period during the Episcopacy of Presiding Bishop Henry Knox Sherrill from 1949 to 1958 as the age of the national church ideal. In this age the Episcopal Church came to see itself as "a light to the nations." Douglas quotes M. B. Gill, who saw the missionary work of the Episcopal Church as an American effort "to Christianize the Monroe Doctrine." It was in this mindset that many of the members of the Episcopal Church who lived outside the United States found themselves participating in efforts meant not only to evangelize them to the gospel but also to American principles of democracy and capitalism.

There is no denying that across the globe, Christian missionary efforts moved hand-in-hand with national colonial efforts. Sometimes this missionary zeal was pervaded with chauvinism, racism, and bigotry, and many suffered as a result of this kind of violence and abuse in the name of religion. While we cannot deny that there was an element of American colonialism to Episcopal mission efforts, Lamin Sanneh warns us that we can overstate the level of control and sometimes overgeneralize the oppressive nature of modern Christian missionary efforts by painting all missionaries with the same brush. While Americans, and other nations as well, wanted to promote American style democracy and build vast global economic empires, true evangelism was also a genuine goal of modern missionary efforts. To see missionary energies as simply colonialism carried out through the auspices of the church undermines the truth of how even the colonial period of missionary efforts, when accompanied by translation work, opened the doors for new expressions of spiritual identity within evangelized regions.

Once the gospel is put in the hands of peoples hearing it in their own native languages, control becomes impossible. As it had since Christianity's beginnings, the gospel took on its own life. Through translation efforts, missionaries opened the door for new Christians to help shape what the church was to become. By supporting biblical and liturgical translation and thereby moving away from its English-speaking roots, the Episcopal Church in mission areas took on its own expression, its own color, its own cultural foundation. Even in settings where economic and cultural control were part of the dynamic supporting these missionary efforts, translation by its very nature subverts control. When liturgies and scripture were translated into other tongues, not only were the lives of people in missionary regions changed by introduction to Christianity in its Episcopal form, but Episcopal identity was also reshaped by contact with its newest members. As a result, the English-speaking American church of most of the nineteenth century ceased to exist. Instead, the Episcopal Church in its national church form came to be made up of both its originating dioceses and a plethora of missionary dioceses that stretched across the globe.

With the coming of the liberation movements and theologies of the late twentieth century and the civil unrest of that era in the United States, a skepticism regarding the value of a national church paradigm ushered in a new vision for what mission might mean. By the late twentieth century, our understanding of mission had, Douglas tells us, moved to a less paternalistic model of mutuality that celebrated more fully the values of self-government, self-support, and self-propagation. When the international Anglican Congress met in 1963, they issued a paper titled "Mutual Responsibility and Interdependence in the Body of Christ." In that paper they wrote, "The keynotes of our time are equality, interdependence, mutual responsibility." This new global vision for Anglicanism was about partnership, and the language that came to be used to describe Episcopal missionary relationships was "Partners in Mission," implying a level of mutuality that was not always present in earlier eras.

This changed understanding of mission reminds us that the work of translation, whether it is the translation of scripture, of liturgical rites, or of pietistic practices is a give-and-take process with both entities being stretched and changed by the encounter. Translation often leads to new insights, to new priorities, and to new perspectives as communities move from a fixed understanding of the meaning of a spiritual concept to a reinvigoration of that concept with new images, metaphors, or a different weighting of the central message given through an encounter with a less dominant culture. Much of our expanded vision of what it means to be a Christian and an Episcopalian has developed over the last decades since the 1979 Book of Common Prayer as we have lived in this Episcopal global community of mutual love and respect.

This kind of respectful partnership has historically offered Christianity the opportunity to reinvent itself over and over again. A small band of Jewish followers of Jesus took Christianity from Jerusalem and Galilee out into the larger Hellenistic Jewish diaspora, then into the Hellenistic world, the Roman Empire, and across the earth through two millennia. Treasuring diversity of thought and experience is part of the hallmark of the history of Christianity. It is also a core value expressed again for our day in resolution 9 of A068. The resolution implicitly affirms that the church is most vital when it declares that the gospel belongs equally to all people of all languages, cultures, and races: this is when we are living most fully into our eschatological identity. To claim this truth and celebrate it is to open the church up to the riches of wisdom, knowledge, and experience that can be shared by a church that sees itself as part of a global community rather than a national church temporarily supporting dependent missionary partners. In a global community, all members must be full members, respected members, who have the right to speak and to pray in the prayer language of their hearts and through the customs, traditions, and gestures that ground their identity.

We can and should translate our traditional Americanized, English language rites into the many languages of Episcopalians, but translation cannot simply mean taking words written by English speakers and transliterating them into other languages. Anyone who has learned a foreign language knows that one of the great gifts that language brings is not just a way to interact with others who do not speak our language, but also a way to see our own world through different eyes.

In earlier prayer book revisions, our efforts to acknowledge and respect the multilingual nature of our Episcopal identity often fell short. Rather than inviting Spanish-speaking Episcopalians to translate Episcopal liturgies to meet their needs, or Taiwanese Episcopalians to create liturgies that carried the core of Episcopal liturgical expression but communicated in a quintessentially Taiwanese way, we gave them stilted authorized translations formed by native English speakers. Translations that did not resonate with the rhythms, sensibilities, and aesthetics of the people they were to be used by. Instead, these transliterations often served as a regular reminder that officially the church still saw normative Episcopal worship, at its heart, as a part of English-language-based, North American, Euro-centered culture. Now we know better. Now we know the power of true translation to bless the lives of all Episcopalians.

One principle that is important in this work is the value of looking for dynamic equivalents. Dynamic equivalency is a terminology developed by liturgical scholar Anscar Chapungco of the Philippines. It is an inculturation principle that says that when translating rites, one must look for the image, metaphor, or expression that has the capacity to carry a similar message and weight of message as the piece of the tradition one is trying to share.

What is the dynamic equivalent of bread in Honduras or Taiwan or Micronesia? What metaphor has the power to communicate to people, in a different corner of the world than English-speaking America, that Christ is the substance that can sustain our lives? What music speaks of joy and sorrow in another cultural context? What colors and symbols resonate in the deep consciousness of our brothers and sisters who have spent their lives immersed in something other than Western European music, art, and literature? How will all our lives be changed if we receive images of Mary as a Native American or Christ as a Latino? If our altars are covered in grass weavings rather than brocade? If in some communities the primary musical instrument of worship is a drum not an organ? If our sermons must reach into the hearts of not one but two or more linguistic and cultural communities? Louis Weil's work of the beginning of this new millennium has already invited us to begin to address many of these important questions. Inculturation of the Episcopal tradition asks us to move beyond the familiar and the literal to find the best way possible to share the faith we hold in common.

By including this particular section in the resolution to move forward with liturgical renewal, the Episcopal Church of 2018 asserted that we believe that mutuality, mutual valuation and respect, diversity, and contextuality are all important and positive aspects to who we are as Episcopalians. Bringing this attitudinal framework into the way we worship will bless and strengthen our church and our church's relationship to the broader culture. Part of the work of the task force will be to find ways to embrace this value by inviting all of us to share aspects of our own culture and at the same time invite all of us to claim the richness of our shared identity by embracing in our own worship others' linguistic, ethnic, cultural, and national expressions of faith.

This commitment to a broader vision of who we are will inevitably call us to address theological and pietistic questions in a way that does not require that we all come to the same understandings or the same liturgical actions. Most likely as we address these questions, we will have the opportunity to reshape our rites in a way that expresses the realities of contemporary life in a less standardized, more elastic way. Perhaps our common life will grow not so much out of our saying the same words or singing the same hymns as sharing the same vision for the world and proclaiming the same Lord. Unity does not have to mean uniformity, and indeed church historians can witness to the countless ways in which even when official church laws required uniformity in the words, the experiences of congregations across the globe were dramatically different because of the aesthetic, emotional, gestural, and cultural eccentricities of the community in which those rites were being celebrated.

In some parts of the Episcopal Church, our life together is already overflowing with a bounty of riches created by diverse ages, ethnicities, and cultures sharing life in a faith community. Having served in a church where there were fourteen different original nationalities represented by the church members, it becomes clear that to truly celebrate who we are, we must honor the traditions that have made us who we are. This may be as simple an act as placing a statue or painting of Our Lady of Guadalupe in our sanctuary. It may mean offering additional new rites that speak to cultural traditions regarding birth, death, and marital anniversaries. Inevitably musical choices reflect our respect for one another's sense of beauty, and the emotional tenor of our services speaks as much to our familial and cultural backgrounds as to our Episcopal identity.

The Episcopal Church of the twenty-first century is so much more than a national church, and it is much more than an English-speaking church. Fewer and fewer of its members have ties to English history other than the ties that grow out of our knowledge of our historical background as a member of the Anglican Communion with an identity that began through Church of England missions to the Americas. As we move deeper into this century's era of liturgical renewal, may we all work to find the means to open ourselves to new voices and new perspectives. May our ritual life celebrate the diverse strength and beauty that makes the Episcopal Church the church it is today.

Questions for Discussion

1. Share your own cultural and ethnic background. What might your own culture offer to the broader church to make its life richer?
2. Share a holiday, festival, or feast day that you especially resonate with, and explain why this is so meaningful to you.

3. If our liturgical life were to become a fuller celebration of cultural diversity, how might that look in concrete terms?
4. Share an experience you have had with someone of a different cultural background than you, and how that enriched your life.
5. Explore this Anglican principle from "Mutual Responsibility and Interdependence in the Body of Christ:" "The keynotes of our time are equality, interdependence, mutual responsibility." Does this principle still hold today? How might this find expression in our worship life?

5
Diversity and Common Worship

RUTH A. MEYERS

IN 2006, THE General Convention approved *Changes*, a collection of rites of passage that the Standing Commission on Liturgy and Music had developed. Designed for both corporate worship and family use, the rites mark transitions in human life, expressing "confidence in God's presence among us throughout the changes and chances of this life" ("Theology and Rationale," *Changes*, 2007).

The materials in this collection reflect the cultural, racial, and ethnic diversity of the Episcopal Church, recognizing that different cultures celebrate events in the human life cycle in distinctive ways. For example, in many Latin American communities, a girl celebrates her fifteenth birthday with a *Quinceañera* (Spanish: "fifteen years"), and *Changes* includes "A Rite of Passage for a Significant Birthday." Some cultures have a practice of formally naming elders, so *Changes* provides "A Rite for the Blessing or Commissioning of an Elder." In many parts of the United States, earning a driver's license or permit marks a significant transition in a teen's development, and *Changes* includes a prayer for use on this occasion.

In the prayers and liturgies in *Changes*, cultural practices and Christian worship intersect. However, the interplay between Christian worship and culture is not limited to rites that mark life-cycle transitions. Christian worship is always celebrated in specific cultural contexts, creating a dynamic relationship between worship and culture.

During the 1990s, the Lutheran World Federation held a series of consultations on worship and culture, bringing together an ecumenical group of scholars and church leaders from different regions of the world. Their work resulted in the 1996 Nairobi Statement, which identified different ways in which Christian worship and culture intersect:

> Christian worship relates dynamically to culture in at least four ways. First, it is transcultural, the same substance for everyone everywhere, beyond culture. Second, it is contextual, varying according to the local situation (both nature and culture). Third, it is counter-cultural, challenging what is contrary to the Gospel in a given culture. Fourth, it is cross-cultural, making possible sharing between different local cultures. (Lutheran World Federation, 1.3)

As liturgical and prayer book revision proceeds in the Episcopal Church, attention to each of these aspects of worship and culture will enable development of liturgies that draw upon the diversity of our church.

Transcultural

All Christian worship responds to the triune God, who is revealed in the life, death, and resurrection of Jesus Christ and who sends the Holy Spirit. Some Christian practices transcend distinct cultural expressions. We become Christian through baptism with water, a practice rooted in Christ and handed down through the centuries. Christians throughout the world celebrate the eucharistic meal, following Jesus's command to "do this in remembrance of me." Christians share the proclamation of scripture and the use of the Lord's Prayer in their assemblies for worship, although translations vary.

Episcopalians are united in our use of The Book of Common Prayer. From its origins in sixteenth-century England, the BCP was introduced around the world as the British Empire expanded. The prayer book, sometimes described as the glue holding the Anglican Communion together, made Anglican worship transcultural, that is, extending beyond all cultures, even as it was translated into different languages.

By the twentieth century, churches of the Anglican Communion were developing prayer books suitable for their own contexts, and it became clear that the singular use of the sixteenth century was no longer possible. Beginning in the 1980s, the International Anglican Liturgical Consultation has worked to identify norms of Anglican worship, developing principles and making recommendations to the churches of the Anglican Communion. The 1995 consultation on the Eucharist proposed that unity is expressed through structure rather than a single common text.

In the Episcopal Church, the 1979 Book of Common Prayer had already moved away from a single uniform text for the Eucharist. Yet the structure remains constant. Both Rite I and Rite II follow the sequence of actions in "An Order for Celebrating the Holy Eucharist" (BCP, 400–401), balancing proclamation of the word, intercessory prayer, and the eucharistic meal. This common structure means that an Episcopalian will find a familiar flow of worship when visiting any Episcopal Church in any diocese. In addition, the use of the Revised Common Lectionary, which became the Lectionary of the BCP in 2007, unites Episcopalians with many churches of the Anglican Communion and with Protestant churches throughout the world that have adopted this pattern of scripture readings across a three-year cycle.

Though not universal among all Christians, both the common structure of the Eucharist and the common lectionary are significant transcultural aspects of worship that help unite Episcopalians in common worship. As worshiping communities create new liturgical texts with the encouragement of Resolution A068, following a common shape of the liturgy will help ensure that our worship is recognizably Anglican and in continuity with Christian tradition.

Beyond the overall structure of the Eucharist, our eucharistic prayers have characteristic elements organized in a pattern that flows from thanksgiving to supplication. Recent eucharistic prayers from around the Anglican Communion use this structure, which is also commended in the 1982 ecumenical document *Baptism, Eucharist, and Ministry*. Crafting new eucharistic prayers that maintain this dynamic of thanksgiving and supplication and incorporate these common elements will offer another important transcultural touchstone.

Contextual

The 1988 Lambeth Conference affirmed the importance of universal norms for Anglican worship while also acknowledging that every province of the Anglican Communion is free to worship in forms appropriate to their own cultural context. A year later, the International Anglican Liturgical Consultation, taking up the question of liturgical inculturation (that is, adapting liturgy to the local culture when that is consistent with the gospel), pointed out that the common prayer of the first Book of Common Prayer was expressed in the culture of its time, particularly in its use of Tudor English. The Episcopal Church claimed a similar freedom in the preface to its first Book of Common Prayer, which stated its intent not to depart from the Church of England in essential doctrine, discipline, or worship, "or further than local circumstances require" (BCP, 11).

The 1979 BCP introduced significant contextualization with the use of contemporary language in the Rite II forms of Daily Offices, Holy Eucharist, and Burial of the Dead, and in most other rites, which is an example of dynamic equivalence. In this method of contextualization, the meanings and actions of worship are expressed in the language and forms of the local culture. A different method, creative assimilation, adds elements from the local culture to enrich the worship. As the Episcopal Church develops liturgies that utilize our diversity, both methods can be employed.

The gathering of the assembly for worship can employ elements of a local culture in several ways. The 1979 BCP allows a hymn, psalm, or anthem to be sung at the beginning of the Eucharist, and this music can reflect the local culture, for example, an African-American congregation singing a spiritual. Similarly, a song of praise used instead of the *Gloria in excelsis* can be a local cultural expression.

As the BCP is revised, it could offer more flexible rubrics and a variety of texts to encourage communities to gather using forms familiar in the local context. The underlying intent of this first movement of worship is to draw the assembly together in praise, preparing them to hear the word, offer their intercessions, and celebrate the eucharistic meal. This could take many forms consistent with Christian teaching. Some Native American communities have introduced a prayer to the four directions when gathering for the Eucharist. A predominantly white congregation in the Midwest moved the exchange of the Peace to the beginning of the liturgy, reflecting cultural practices of welcoming.

The eucharistic prayer can use images familiar in the local context. Eucharistic Prayer C praises God who created "the vast expanse of interstellar space, galaxies, suns, the planets in their courses, and this fragile earth, our island home" (BCP, 370), language that reflects the age of space exploration that began in the mid-twentieth century. A eucharistic prayer from Melanesia praises God who created "these islands, beaches, reefs, mountains, and valleys" and thanks God for "the bush, palm trees, lagoons, and oceans" (Church of the Province of Melanesia, 2011, 314). Such language expresses confidence in God's presence in the midst of the people who are worshiping, inviting them to see God's hand at work in their part of the world. As new eucharistic prayers are written for the Episcopal Church, they can use evocative language and images that encourage Episcopalians to recognize God at work in their contexts.

The prayer book allows contextualization in ways not specified in texts and rubrics. Ceremonial gestures and movement, vestments, architecture, and other nonverbal elements of worship vary from place to place and have changed over the centuries. By leaving much unsaid, the prayer book already creates space for local communities to worship in ways that reflect their cultural context.

A careful review of rubrics might uncover other possibilities. For example, the additional directions for the Eucharist dictate that the celebrant receives first, then the bishops, priests, and deacons at the table, and only after them do the people receive (BCP, 407). Yet in many cultures where the Episcopal Church is located, it is common for the host to eat last, after the guests have been served. Rubrics such as this might be revised to be less restrictive, allowing or even encouraging congregations to adopt a practice that best reflects local culture.

Countercultural

Some cultural practices can be incorporated into Christian worship because they are consistent with the gospel and reflect God's presence within local cultures and communities. But not all cultural practices are in harmony with the gospel. Jesus challenged human practices that are oppressive, dehumanizing, and sinful. His death and resurrection offer transformation.

Intercessory prayer is an important way to challenge injustice and oppression. The 1979 Book of Common Prayer introduced significant developments, broadening the prayers of the people by requiring intercession for "the Nation and all in authority" as well as "the welfare of the world." Some of the six set forms pray explicitly for justice and peace, not limiting the administration of justice to the rulers of the nations. New liturgical texts might provide more options to name oppression and injustice.

Some of the 1979 texts include prayer for the care of creation, reflecting the awareness of environmental degradation that began to emerge during the 1960s. As the BCP is revised, new rubrics might require prayer for the care of creation and the healing of the planet as a standard element in the prayers of the people at the Eucharist. The confession of sin could be explicit about human participation in the pollution and destruction of creation. Some dioceses have proposed adding a question to the Baptismal Covenant eliciting a commitment to care for God's creation.

Liturgical texts that lament and confess injustice are one form of countercultural worship. Resolution A068 calls for the use of inclusive and expansive language and imagery for humanity and divinity, work that has been underway in the Episcopal Church since the

1980s. Inclusive language, for example, referring to "humanity" rather than "mankind," underscores the full and equal dignity of all human beings, countering the oppression of people who are on the margins, systemic sin that has been challenged in recent years by, for example, the Black Lives Matter and Me Too movements. Expansive language endeavors to broaden the language and imagery used to speak about God, drawing from scripture and Christian tradition, and in so doing to shape the identity of the community of faith in a manner that fosters justice and liberation.

Other worship practices may serve to form Christian community in ways that challenge cultural norms that run counter to the gospel. The prayer book requires silence at the breaking of the bread and allows it as well after readings and before the confession of sin. Such silence is a countercultural practice in North America today. Our environment surrounds us with sound, with background music nearly ubiquitous. Silence during many formal presentations or programs is indicative of a mistake. In Christian worship, by contrast, silence can provide space for holy listening, attentive to the still, small voice of God. It invites members of the assembly to set aside the hurried pace of the world, intent on productivity and accomplishment. The 1979 BCP calls for silence in only a few places, and new liturgies could encourage its use in additional places, for example, after the sermon in the Eucharist.

Congregational singing with live accompaniment is also countercultural in the United States. With the rise of recorded music, people may sing along, but rarely does a group of people join in song together, except at a birthday party or the seventh-inning stretch at a baseball game. At some concerts, people will sing, particularly if the performer encourages them. Yet the purpose of a concert is entertainment, often with a price for admission, whereas worship emphasizes participation. Singing together requires listening and breathing together, embodying the assembly's union with God in Christ, challenging the rugged individualism of the predominant white American culture. Revision of the BCP might consider how to encourage congregational singing, adding to the options for use of a hymn, psalm, or anthem already provided in the 1979 BCP.

Cross-cultural

The 1549 Book of Common Prayer was firmly situated in the context of sixteenth-century England, using the Tudor English of its day and relying heavily upon monarchical language to speak to and about God, for example, "thy divine Majesty." The Episcopal Church is far more diverse, and incorporating into worship elements from different cultures can express that richness. Moreover, the Episcopal Church is one small part of the Church universal. Jesus lived, died, and rose for the sake of the world, and he sent his disciples to preach the gospel to all nations. Thoughtful incorporation of elements from different cultures can enrich the church and strengthen its unity in Christ.

Music offers one way to introduce cross-cultural elements into worship. The prayer book is silent about the forms of music, other than stipulating that hymns are authorized by the church and the words of anthems are to be from scripture or the prayer book, or congruent with them (BCP, 14). *The Hymnal 1982* introduced a few hymns from outside white Euro-American cultures, for example, "Lift every voice and sing" (Hymn 599). Later supplements, including *Lift Every Voice and Sing II*; *Wonder, Love, and Praise*; and *El Himnario* provided more extensive selections. As the prayer book is revised, allowing congregations to select music beyond what is officially authorized would enable congregations to enrich their worship with a wide range of music.

Introducing music, as well as other elements from cultures different from those of the congregation, is best done with awareness of and sensitivity to the context of the originating culture. Sometimes it is possible for people from another culture to join a congregation for worship, and music introduced at such times can continue to be part of a congregation's repertoire, embodying common bonds in Christ. Often, however, the introduction of music from different cultures will require a skilled musician to learn how the music is performed in its original context and to teach that to the congregation. Some congregations include people from different cultures, and they can introduce songs to one another to reflect their diversity.

Language can be another significant cross-cultural experience. Some congregations invite worshipers to pray the Lord's Prayer in the language of their heart, and members of the assembly respond with multiple languages prayed simultaneously. The experience of diverse languages prayed together makes the entire assembly aware of both their difference and their unity in Christ.

The *Book of Occasional Services 2018* includes several rites from Mexico and Central America: *Las Posadas* (Spanish: "the inns," a Mexican tradition that commemorates the journey of Mary and Joseph to Bethlehem), *El Dia de los Muertos* (Spanish: "Day of the Dead," celebrated on All Saints' and All Souls' Days, November 1 and 2), and the feast of *La Virgen de Guadalupe* (Spanish: "the Virgin of Guadalupe," a Mexican practice commemorating a vision of the Virgin Mary on December 12). These offer opportunities for cross-cultural experiences for those whose roots are not in those contexts. The rubrics for each of these emphasize that communities for whom these are not culturally indigenous practices should engage in dialogue with communities or individuals for whom they are indigenous as they plan a celebration.

Conclusion

Resolution A068 calls for liturgical and prayer book revision to utilize "our Church's liturgical, cultural, racial, generational, linguistic, gender, physical ability, class and ethnic diversity in order to share common worship." Our Anglican tradition provides a solid foundation for a creative tension that enables diverse communities to worship in common.

The Book of Common Prayer provides forms of worship that transcend diversity of all sorts: one baptism with water in the triune name; a structure for the Eucharist that includes proclamation of the Word, intercessory prayer, and the eucharistic meal, with bread and wine taken, blessed, broken, and shared; a common lectionary. Attention to these transcultural elements in the process of liturgical and prayer book revision will help ensure continuity with Christian tradition and foster a sense of common worship within the Episcopal Church and the Anglican Communion as well as with other Christians.

We also worship in particular ways, reflecting distinct cultural contexts. The language of our worship, the music we sing, our gestures and movement, and the space in which we worship express values and norms of different cultures. Some practices are contextual, part of the local culture's values and patterns and also consonant with the gospel. Other practices are cross-cultural, incorporating elements from different contexts and thereby enriching the congregation, strengthening its ties with Christians in other places and times, and bearing witness to the unity of the Church. In the process of liturgical and prayer book revision, new resources can adapt language and practices from different cultural contexts in the Episcopal Church, enabling worship that will be contextual for some and cross-cultural for others.

While worship is embedded in a local context and incorporates elements of cultures that are in harmony with the gospel, it must also confront and challenge aspects of culture that contradict the gospel. Prayers of intercession and confession may name injustice and oppression directly. Patterns of worship may also engage worshipers in practices that challenge prevailing cultural norms and embody gospel values.

Prayer book revision offers an opportunity for the Episcopal Church to recognize the diversity of its members and their many different cultural contexts. A thorough review of texts and rubrics and judicious revision can lead to practices that reflect our diversity and create space for local communities to incorporate elements from their context, while at the same uniting us in common worship.

Questions for Discussion

1. If you have visited another Episcopal Church or worshiped in another church of the Anglican Communion, what similarities and differences did you notice in their worship?
2. What aspects of worship give you a sense of connection to Christians in other times and places?

3. In the Sunday worship of your home congregation, what practices reflect your local cultural context?
4. What practices in your home congregation are countercultural, challenging aspects of the culture?
5. How does your congregation incorporate elements from other cultures in its worship?

6

Can Anglican Liturgy Be Universal?

Juan M. C. Oliver

Introduction

In 2018 the General Convention of the Episcopal Church called for additional liturgical resources originating beyond the dominant culture to be included in the revised Book of Common Prayer and the Book of Occasional Services. This naturally brings up the matter of the relationship between Anglican liturgy and cultures beyond the Anglo mainstream, for so far almost all Anglican liturgical practice and theology has taken place in the Anglo context, or simply exported abroad wholesale through colonial efforts. Although the Prayer Books of Brazil, New Zealand, and Spain are very worthy exceptions, this presents a challenge to the Anglican claim to be a catholic, that is, universal, Church, as it does not reflect the whole gamut of its membership.

In what follows I explore some elements of the relationship between an Anglican liturgy and the culture(s) in which it finds itself. I will be referring to other cultures from the mainstream, but in fact, the relationship of Anglican liturgy to even Anglo culture(s) applies as well. I begin from H. Richard Niebuhr's position that the Church is called to transform culture, neither completely identifying with nor abandoning it. I then explore how ritual works as a system of sign-actions presenting a felt and understood experience of our vision of the coming reign of God. Looking more closely, I then examine liturgy as a system of signs that effect an invisible, interior grace and how, as signs, they must convey meaning not only to the universal Church over the centuries, but to the culturally situated persons participating in it today. I conclude with a summary and a glimmer of hope.

Church, Liturgy, and Culture(s)

Church and Culture(s)

Our understanding of the nature of the Church (ecclesiology) affects our understanding of the Church's liturgy. For brevity's sake I will embrace at the outset H. Richard Niebuhr's view proposed in his *Christ and Culture*: Christ's (and therefore the Church's) relationship to culture is *transformative*. Thus, the Christian *ekklesia* (assembly) is not merely an uncritical extension of the culture in which it finds itself, nor can it hold itself, nose pinched, entirely away from culture.

Christians must live in our cultures, though like leaven in dough, we are called to both support and confront them to cooperate with God's gracious will to give us the reign. This, of course, immediately presents the question of what we mean by the reign of God. By the term, the New Testament means the whole range of meanings in the original Greek: God's kingship, kingdom, sovereignty, reign, and royal power both as a geographic area and as God's authority over it. British bishop and New Testament scholar N. T. Wright, in his essay "Being in the Kingdom Today," makes it clear that the phrase refers to *this* world as God would have it, *here on earth:*

> So many people—I myself thought this when I was younger—assume that when Jesus talks about inheriting the kingdom of heaven, he means going to heaven when you die. . . . That is completely wrong. Jesus taught us to pray in Matthew's Gospel in Chapter 6, "Thy kingdom come; Thy will be done, on earth as in heaven." The phrase kingdom of heaven is not about a place

called heaven, which is somewhere else, where God is king and where we'll go one day. It is about the establishment of the rule of heaven, in other words, the rule of God here on earth.

The Church, then, lives in expectation of a new world ruled by God—a world transfigured by justice, peace, and love; a healed ("saved") world restored to our original nature as images of God. To some of my generation it may come as a surprise to hear that the Church is to transform its surrounding culture. Seven decades ago our cultures—both North American Anglo and Latin American—were at least nominally Christian, but increasingly, many cultures no longer embody a Christian worldview and practice.

Liturgy and Culture

In the midst of our fallen world, the Christian assembly gathers to worship God. Through the instrumentality of the gathered Church, God acts to further the work of sanctification, salvation, healing, and transformation of all creation into God's reign. This takes place in worship through the congregation's sign-actions. I employ "sign-action" rather than simply "sign" because the sacraments are not simply objects, but things made sacred in the context of our sacred *doings*. The consecrated elements in the Eucharist, for example, depend on the sign-action that is praying the Great Thanksgiving in order to be body and blood of Christ.

From the outset, even before the gospel is proclaimed, our gathering for the work of God is in tension with the human culture(s) in which it takes place; this tension is *always* inherent in the liturgical action, which presents a vision of the *coming* reign of God, as if it were to arrive *here and now*: a vision acted out by a congregation that has been, consciously or not, shaped by its specific culture.

Precisely because it proclaims an envisioned reign of God and equips the assembly with the values, attitudes, and dispositions to live in it, liturgy embodies a tension between the world as it is and how it would be under God's gracious rule. This means, in turn, that unlike other rituals of humanity, *Christian* liturgy not only preserves culture, but also challenges it to be all that it is called to be by God, while confronting its fallen aspects. It does not merely support or bless the existing social order; it also undermines it and challenges it by rehearsing a vision of the reign of God.

Liturgy as Signifying Action

The catechism definition of a sacrament, "a visible external sign of an invisible interior grace," has been with us since the fourth century, if not earlier. The ancients, however, were not very interested in *how*. Practically all theological writing on the sacraments until the eighth century revels in the parallelism between a sign and what it means, never explaining *how* it brings about grace in the participants. It was enough for them to note, for example, that by the conclusion of the great Amen, the bread on the altar was the body of Christ—never mind how. This parallelism between sign and signified was already there in Paul's Letter to the Romans all along: "For if we have been planted [or grown] together [with the Anointed] in/through a likeness of his death, we shall at least also be [in the likeness of] the resurrection" (Rom. 6:5, translation mine). And so, almost three hundred years after Paul, Cyril of Jerusalem would marvel, in his Catechetical Lecture (20:5):

> Oh strange and inconceivable thing! We did not really die, we were not really buried, we were not really crucified and raised again; but our imitation was in a figure, and our healing in reality. Christ was actually crucified, and actually buried, and truly rose again; and all these things He has freely bestowed upon us, that we, sharing His sufferings by imitation, might gain salvation in reality.

And so the ordinary human actions that make up liturgy have an *analogical* relationship to the grace received by the participants. As a candidate for baptism is immersed in water and comes back up to breathe, she is also interiorly buried and risen again to new life. This analogical relationship between the sign and what is signified is not an abstraction, but something perceived, felt, and understood by a person in a specific cultural context. And this brings up the question of *meaning.*

Meaning

As signs, the sacraments and, indeed, all ritual actions of the Christian assembly *mean.* That is, as exterior sign-acts, they *mediate* an interior grace. The fact that they mean is of their *essence,* for a sign that does not mean is no sign. Aquinas wrote that the sacraments *effect* what they mean *by meaning it.* And so, for example, immersion, meaning death and rebirth, effects the new life of grace.

In order to mean, however, the sign-actions must be either so universal as to be easily recognizable across all cultures, or else they must be carried out in the cultural language of the participants—not only verbal language but all the other communicative elements in worship: body language, gestures, movement, spatial arrangement, decoration, music, and silence as well as words. For it would not do—indeed, it would be absurd—to claim, for example, that we are reborn to new life by having the candidate go up, say, in a hot air balloon. *The analogy is not there.* And so, regardless of how much hot air is available, no grace can be effected in the candidate—unless of course sending someone up into the sky were a sign of starting a new life in that local culture. This is because the meaning of signs is never isolated, existing by itself, unrelated to anything else; for meaning is always meaning-to-someone, and that someone is always a culturally shaped person.

The members of concrete Christian congregations at prayer exist in specific human cultures, with their values, forms of expression, worldview, ethos, and so on. There are never "universal people" at worship. In practice this means that the church community is *never* without its cultural context(s). The assembly may be Anglo, Latino, Polish, Native American, or Zimbabwean; it may be mostly poor, or wealthy, or middle class, literate or not, but always and everywhere it is already formed by cultural notions and expressions of things like reverence, respect, awe, praise, petition, sacrality, and authority—to name but a few. They are never a blank slate.

Types of Signs and How They Mean

It is helpful, I think, to differentiate among kinds of liturgical sign-actions on the basis of how they mean and to whom: *universal* signs, *culturally specific* signs, and *individual, private* signs.

Universal signs are basic human actions like eating, drinking, bathing, touching—so basic that all humans can easily recognize them *if they are unabridged.* Sharing bread and wine in thanksgiving for Jesus's life, death, and resurrection in a dinner church in twenty-first-century Brooklyn today means approximately the same thing as it did to a community in first-century Corinth.

Culturally specific signs, however, may have to be explained to people outside the culture where they originated. It may not be so wise, for example, for a Christian man to attempt to embrace an Arab woman at the Peace, unless he is her husband. His hug would not be a sign of peace to her, but a sign of disrespect or even harassment. Individual, private signs, in turn, are signs to a specific person, and not shared much more widely. A spouse's photograph, for example, carries meaning to the spouse who recognizes it, but none in particular for someone who finds it on the street.

We should recall, however, that official and doctrinal meanings were originally shared individual meanings, brought together through dialogue, church councils, and so on. It seems wise, therefore, to always consider the meaning of a liturgical sign-action under three lenses:

1. *Universal meaning.* Examples of this might be the core sign-actions of the Eucharist: gathering, listening to God's word, sharing or applying its meaning, praying, offering, giving thanks, eating together, and being sent out on mission. As long as these actions are clear and unabridged, the participants of any culture may be reasonably expected to be aware of their meaning—immediately and without explanation.
2. *Local expression.* How and what the actions mean to the local culturally positioned participants. Do they mean the same as the universal meaning? If not, they may need to take place in

a manner appropriate to the local cultural context. How do people in this specific cultural context gather, listen, share, pray, offer, and so on? Implementing the answers well, we may reasonably expect them to carry meaning to these people, whether an Anglo suburban congregation or an inner-city Chinese assembly or a Hispanic congregation in New Mexico.

3. *Individual appropriation.* The meaning of the sign-actions to the individual participants. This may vary widely. It is important, moreover, that this personal meaning *not* be the *final* criterion for liturgical decision-making. "Our daughter's baptism meant for us that that she was connected to Grandma by wearing her christening gown" is a fine personal sentiment, but it is not the meaning of baptism in our tradition. Sometimes individual meanings may veer off even to the point of not being Christian at all. In my essay "Worship, Forming and Deforming," I have named this the *deformative* aspect of liturgical actions that remain so opaque that the participants project meanings on them that are simply not there, for example, as when a confirmand says that in that rite she is "joining the Episcopal Church." The *rite* says no such thing, though it may well be its meaning *for her.*

In sum, the liturgy's sign-actions effect what they signify as signs *within* the cultural context of the assembly, universally, locally, and individually.

Catechesis

What if the sign does not mean anything to the assembly, should we discard it? Yes and no. As a series of sign-acts, liturgy requires from its participants the ability to "read" the signs. The more universal the sign is—bathing, for example—the less explanation it needs. The more arcane and specific (the *lavabo*, for example), the more explanation it may need. People—even clergy—have a tendency to call this explication of unknown arcana "catechesis," meaning by that term, for example, having to explain that hosts are bread, or what a corporal is, or the right liturgical color to use. The early church, however, did not employ particularly obscure sign-actions. There were no hosts, but bread, a linen cloth was just that, and liturgical colors were still far in the future. Their catechesis consisted of a different and much deeper process: allowing the Word to resound in the ears of baptismal candidates, moving them to conversion of life, and after their baptism, helping them delve into the meaning of the sign-actions and their meanings in our tradition and to them. Thus catechesis in the early church did not explain obscure sign-acts or sign-objects as much as it opened the eyes of the new members to recognize that in baptism they had been "buried" with Christ and risen to new life, as members of his risen body and to recognize him at "the breaking of bread"—our shared meal, in both the bread on the table and in the gathered congregation.

The Incarnation of Worship in Cultures

So what may change and what must not? Is a Christian community to design its worship from scratch, as if our history had never taken place? Or should a local church own some core aspects of the tradition that, in turn, inform what may or may not be changed?

Unchanging Elements

There are core, universal aspects of Christian worship. For example, our liturgy has generally been directed to the first person of the Trinity, through the second, in the third. Further, our liturgy, as the body of the risen Christ, has always been Christological: it refers to and indeed embodies Christ—all that he was, did, said, and preached—and its inevitable consequence: his arrest, torture, and execution, followed by God's vindication, raising him from the dead and sending the Spirit upon the Church to announce the Good News to all nations. These are only two examples of universal elements in Christian worship—regardless of denomination or culture.

And Anglicans? One might expect that since we acknowledge only the councils of the first seven centuries we might not have *any* of our own traits as a tradition, but we do. There are some cross-cultural, universal characteristics of our liturgy found in any liturgies that bear the adjective "Anglican."

The first two are a question of our relationship to Canterbury: Is the congregation, through its bishop, in communion with the see of Canterbury? And, is this liturgy led by persons ordained (or received) by Anglican bishops? The third is scriptural: Is the liturgy based on the biblical treasure house that we have inherited? The fourth is cultural: Is this liturgy in the language spoken by the people—not only the verbal language, but the myriad nonverbal ways of communicating, such as the arrangement of the place of worship and our actions, objects, music, and silences as well as words? Finally, aesthetic: Is the liturgy beautiful and conducted decently and in order?

Most of the criteria I just listed may be easily ascertained, except the last one. The love of beauty, reverence, decency, and order are surely universal—no one would admit to preferring ugly, irreverent, indecent, and disordered rites—but the ways in which these values are expressed are always culturally specific. When a Latino congregation in Puerto Rico, for example, claps and sings, moving to a beat, to welcome the Gospel, it *is* being reverent. An African village bringing up all manner of agricultural produce—even live chickens—in the presentation of the gifts at the Eucharist *is* being decent and orderly. A Guatemalan assembly of impoverished peasants decorating with faded plastic flowers *does* consider them beautiful. Thus beauty, reverence, decency, and order, unlike the more universal traits mentioned above, are always such in the shared eyes of the beholders: in their cultural, linguistic, social, and sometimes even economic context.

This is why employing one's own taste in worship to judge others' sense of liturgical appropriateness is so fraught with danger. It is like claiming that people who do not speak English are somehow profoundly wrong—a strategy for a put-down. For important though having values of taste and beauty are in Anglican liturgy, one's own notions of beauty, reverence, decency, and order cannot be applied universally. When we do that, we are trying to make others more like ourselves. And this brings me to the colonial record of what we mean by Anglican liturgy.

Anglican Liturgy and the Liturgy of the English

One of the great examples of worship crafted in the tension between gospel and culture was Tudor liturgy. There and then the unchangeable aspects of Christian liturgical meaning were incarnated—not only in the still fresh and developing English language, but in nonverbal ways as well: trestle tables for the Eucharist, almost secular vestments, bread rather than hosts, communicants standing or kneeling around the Holy Table, to name but a few. It did not stop there. In the seventeenth century, the Caroline divines, especially William Laud, and later the Oxford movement further incarnated Anglican liturgy in British culture and mores. Indeed, some of the principles of this process of incarnating the liturgy in England are still valuable guidelines for its incarnation in other cultures.

In the nineteenth century, however, as the world fell to colonization by European powers, the liturgy of the Church of England was exported wholesale. What adaptations of Anglican worship took place in foreign contexts were largely limited to the translations of texts, while the *experience* of worship—its feel, if you will, continued to be British. In many places it still is.

Not everyone, though, bought into this wholesale colonial imposition of British liturgy on the rest of the world. Roland Allen, for example, wrote extensively beginning in 1912 challenging the church to take local cultures seriously as a necessary component of any serious and successful mission. Closer to our time, the International Anglican Liturgical Consultation meeting at York declared:

> This Conference (a) recognizes that culture is the context in which people find their identity; (b) affirms that . . . the gospel judges every culture . . . challenging some aspects of the culture while endorsing others for the benefit of the Church and the society; (c) urges the church everywhere to work at expressing the unchanging gospel of Christ in words, actions, names, customs, liturgies which communicate relevantly in each society.

Who Decides What?

If the incarnation of Anglican liturgy in a specific cultural environment and local cultural modes of expression is desired, whose responsibility is it? The canonical answer is easy: the General Convention or Synod of an Anglican Province. But what does a Church Convention made up of largely white middle-class Anglo Americans know about how Guatemalan immigrants worship?

It is tempting to assume that the priest in charge of the congregation will be responsible for this. At least that is the canonical expectation, and it works (or should) when priest and people share the same cultural context. But if not? How does a priest invite, recognize, and support the laity as they assist her in liturgical planning and design? That is the subject of a more pastoral article, but I can furnish a hint here: acknowledge your own cultural ignorance openly. Help will emerge.

If you build it, they may not come

I am often asked whether a priest should design liturgy in the absence of any others to attract them. I always answer "no." That would be putting the cart before the horse. To design worship in order to attract people as if they were customers belies a consumerist mindset and misses the nature of the Church, which according to the New Testament, is a community, a city, a family, a nation, that is, a group of people, a social body. We are *never* described as a store, or a business—not even a nonprofit corporation—but as the *family of God*. So we must build relationships first, and once a significant proportion of others joins the assembly, learn from them the details of how they worship in their cultures.

For attracting people nothing works better than living out the gospel of the reign through tangible local witness in deeds and not only words. Before thinking of incarnating the liturgy to attract others, therefore, find a deacon if you do not already have one, and give her the charge to discover the real needs of the neighborhood and organize the parish to address them in concerted, long-term ways as witnesses to the coming reign. People will begin to come by, curious. As they begin to belong, (as soon as possible) start asking, *How would you—?* They will be shy, unbelieving that so soon their voice is being encouraged. Insist. If for whatever reason you cannot make room for the ideas suggested or requested, face the fact that your parish is not truly ready to welcome the other. For the other is not your customer; she is your long-lost relative, and yes, she comes in with her culture.

Another reason for not incarnating the liturgy in cultures other than your own is the issue of cultural appropriation. Cultural expressions belong to a specific people. And yet, the American educated class generally values cultural expressions from elsewhere. It is not only a point of pride, but a sign that we are sensitive to the other. So, be careful, but not afraid. For example, in the new *Book of Occasional Services,* the rubrics for such celebrations as Our Lady of Guadalupe and Day of the Dead call for these services to be designed and led by people native to Mexican cultures. If they are absent, you can of course celebrate the rites, but be ready to be confronted.

Liturgical Colonialism Today

I fear that we have such predetermined ideas about appropriate liturgy (appropriate *for U.S. Anglos,* that is) that the moment we step into the world of others whether, say, Newyoricans or Appalachian miners, we immediately want to impose what is meaningful to *us* on *them.* It is no wonder that many a parish trying to "include the other" limps along. The other does not want to be invited in to warm pews.

The agent of inculturation, then, is ultimately the gathered congregation. What aspects of worship might take flesh in their culture(s) while still employing the BCP? As a system of sign-acts, the liturgy includes bodies acting in space and time, and so, our actions involve physical movement, gestures, a place of worship, however temporary, its decoration and arrangement, objects—major or not—music, silences, and, of course, words. All of these, except the words of the rite may be incarnated to express local culture(s). Together, they should cohere to support the core significant actions of worship. If the congregation is bi- or even multicultural, the modes of expression may be mixed; otherwise, the operative criterion still remains, even in the case of Anglo-American congregations: Is this how *these people* envision doing these actions together when God's reign arrives *here*?

The Kenosis of Anglicanism

Is the reader feeling a little uncomfortable by now? Part of our current challenge is that many who may read this will assume *they* are the agent for the inculturation of Anglican worship in cultures other than their own. If I were to remind them that they are probably not, they may be disappointed, hurt, and even angry at the news that they may only be able to support a process led by others.

Further—and perhaps even more anxiety producing—is the possibility that some of their favorite modes of liturgical expression may change, disappear, and go the way of the tried and true, but no longer desired. Things beloved and considered "Anglican" may have to be let go. To some extent this will be an exercise in giving up power. Perhaps we, as a church, might heed the advice of St. Paul to the Phillippians as he describes the self-emptying (*kenosis*), of Christ:

> But be of that mind in yourselves which was also in the Anointed One, Jesus who, subsisting in God's form, did not deem being on equal terms with God a thing to be grasped, but instead, emptied himself, taking a slave's form, coming to be in the likeness of human beings; and, being found as a human being in shape, he reduced himself. . . . (Phil. 2:5–8; Hart 2017)

Conclusion

If the Church is to transform culture(s), we will have to understand *how* liturgy works as a system of sign-actions presenting an eschatological vision of the coming reign of God. Our exterior, visible sign-actions effect interior grace by meaning it and therefore must mean, not only to the universal Church over the centuries, but to the culturally situated persons participating in it today.

So can Anglican liturgy be universal? Perhaps. I hope the answer is "yes." It will largely depend, I wager, on whether Anglican liturgy is ready to empty itself of itself. Are we? Is your local congregation with ten African Americans in it? Is the diocese of Cuba? Is the Province of

Melanesia? To what extent is our own liturgical knowledge, practice, and theology inescapably Anglo? To what extent, in which contexts, and how might we grow and develop ever wider and diverse expressions of Anglican liturgy?

If we cannot do this, I fear we must accept the fact that Anglican liturgy is culturally bound, by nature British, unable to respond to existential cultural situations beyond its own origins, and thus *not* universal—not catholic.

Questions for Discussion

1. Have you participated in liturgies that originate or are celebrated in places other than the Anglo cultural world? What differences did you observe?
2. How do you envision people gathering and listening to the Word, then sharing its meaning in the coming reign of God?
3. In the same coming reign, how, in your vision of it, do people bring offerings, give thanks, and share a meal?
4. How are they sent out with authority to transform society?
5. Do you think Anglican liturgy can be universal? How? Why?

7

Initiated but Unfinished

*Catechetical Foundations for
Fine-Tuning the Baptismal Rite*

WILLIAM H. PETERSEN

Introduction

Over the past forty years, Episcopalians have benefitted from the rite of Holy Baptism in the BCP 1979. Scholarship—in roughly twenty-year intervals—has characterized the rite as a *recovery* (Hatchett 1981, 251–66), a *reformation* (Meyers 1997), and a *revolution* (Turrell 2018). Meanwhile, several specific proposals for further revision of the BCP 1979 have been set forth. Such works are intended to enhance liturgical renewal in the church's life and mission. And "fine-tuning" the rite of Holy Baptism is included among these efforts (Alexander 2000, 3).

Preparing for Baptism

Among the many aspects of the 1979 BCP's Baptismal Rite that can be considered under the category of "recovery," two items particularly stand out. The first of these is the reassertion of baptism as a public liturgy. This recovery set the norm for celebrating baptism principally within the Great Vigil and First Eucharist of Easter and secondarily within the Eucharist on specific Sundays or other Feasts of Our Lord. (The Book of Common Prayer spells this out, specifically on pages

298 and 312.) These days, fewer and fewer Episcopalians can remember a time when baptism was not a public liturgy rather than a private service, as was often the case prior to the 1979 BCP. More often than not, private baptisms occurred either late Sunday afternoon or at the convenience of only the attending parents and godparents of an infant present with the priest. These baptisms could also occur in the parents' residence with extended family and friends in attendance, thus underscoring the rite as a familial "naming" event rather than an ecclesial sacrament.

Perhaps the one positive note in all this was that it could be expected that the parents and perhaps even the godparents were participating and supporting members of the local Christian community in the parish and that the christened infant would be raised in that context. In other words, both age-appropriate theological education and formation in faithful practice would continue as the child matured.

Increasingly, during the latter half of the twentieth century in America these assumptions did not hold. To be sure, relatively newborn children would continue to be presented for baptism, but the contextual opportunity for catechesis diminished. Concomitantly, the period witnessed a small growth in the number of adult persons—raised perhaps within the patina of a Christian culture, but otherwise unchurched and never baptized. This development raised an entirely new set of questions about *recovering* a catechesis, or program of education and formation, more like that of the early Church, that is, a prebaptismal catechesis. This, indeed, was provided for in the years of preparation and trial usage preceding the 1979 BCP, but with all the other reformation and revolution implied by the Baptismal Rite, the catechetical aspects involved were absent from the BCP itself, being relegated to the *Book of Occasional Services.*

All this is simply to recognize that although the 1979 Baptismal Rite presumes an adult baptism, the statistical norm remains much the same as it was formerly. In other words, the 1979 rite assumes that the only theological justification for infant baptism is the baptismal commitment of the parents and sponsors. In contrast to this is the cultural situation that the greatest number of those presented for baptism continue to be primarily infants of baptized-but-nonparticipating parents.

To use our categories and the reflections of liturgical theologian James Turrell (Pritchard 2018), the 1979 Baptismal Rite helped us recover a sacramental practice, reform our understanding of the nature and structure of the Church, and envision a revolution in Christian formation. The first two have largely been accomplished, but the revolution in formation (or catechesis) adequate to the cultural situation has yet to be appropriated for our life and mission.

The central theological revolution of the 1979 Baptismal Rite is the understanding that baptism is not a punctiliar event, but a continuing process. In other words, the "once for all" aspect of baptism as a sacrament does not mean "over and done with" (an event), but rather "initiated and ongoing" (a process). Our baptism into the body of Christ—into his death and resurrection—constitutes a lifelong journey. The early Church made a distinction between pre- and postbaptismal teaching and formation. While the distinction remains important, the more fluid cultural situation of our times practically renders the distinction less absolute. A splendid contemporary and ecumenical resource is provided by the North American Association for the Catechumenate: https://journeytobaptism.org/. To be sure, baptism is a naming ceremony, but the name by which we are designated and the content by which it is endowed through its connection with Jesus Christ only takes on character over time by faithful living in terms of that name. It is significant that the concept "character" derives from the Greek word *carassein,* which means to scratch or mark, hence the distinctive marking of the baptized person at christmation with the mark of Christ, i.e., the cross.

The application of such implications of the ongoing nature of the rite will depend on the commitment of clergy and active laypersons in both the process of prebaptismal teaching and formation in Christian living. (Helpful resources already exist: see, for instance Anne E. Kitch's booklet *Preparing for Baptism in the Episcopal Church*.) What will not suffice is the all-too-frequent practice of merely one or two sessions with either adult candidates or the parents of infants to be presented for baptism.

The revolutionary aspect of such a change in practice was noted twenty years ago by Bishop Neil Alexander when he observed:

> This will demand of those in holy orders a willingness to lay aside much of the work they presently do and rekindle for themselves and for the Church a rabbinical passion for knowing, loving, and living the tradition, not as the repository of our past but as the source of our future. (Meyers 1996)

It is our contention that such a change in practice will not occur unless and until the future Book of Common Prayer includes a section entitled "Preparing for Baptism" that addresses these foundational matters prior to the present section *Concerning the Service*. The single sentence presently appearing as a kind of "afterthought" and mentioning only "instruction in the meaning of Baptism" for parents, godparents, and sponsors without mentioning preliminary "teaching and formation" simply ensures that no change from present practice will occur. A recovered sacramental practice and a reformed baptismal ecclesiology could then be complemented with a revolutionary Christian formation worthy of the reign of God / kingdom of Christ / commonwealth of the Holy Spirit.

Proposing Revisions

> *He [the Father] has rescued us from the power of darkness and transferred us into the kingdom of his beloved Son, in whom we have redemption, the forgiveness of sins.* (Col. 1:13–14, emphasis added)

Perhaps the most astonishing aspect of this passage is its insistence that baptismal living is in terms of the kingdom not just as a future reality in its fulfillment, but as a present fact into which we have been transferred through baptism as the context of our life and mission. Although it will be less astonishing as we now consider our proposed "fine-tunings" of the Baptismal Rite, it will be more practically helpful to set out a comparison of changes in liturgical sequence that will result from these revisions. Thus:

BCP 1979 Order of Service	*Proposed Order of Service*
Presentation of the Candidate(s)	Presentation of the Candidate(s)
Renunciations & Affirmations	Renunciations & Affirmations
Baptismal Covenant	Thanksgiving over the Water
Thanksgiving over the Water	Baptismal Covenant A: Creed
Administration of Water	Administration of Water
Prayer for Gifts of Spirit	Prayer for Gifts of Spirit
Anointing & Marking with Cross	Anointing & Marking with Cross
[Alternate place for Gifts Prayer]	Baptismal Covenant B: Promises
Welcome by the Congregation	Welcome by the Congregation

1. Balance between New Life & Remission of Sin in the Rite

The 1979 Baptismal Rite is particularly commendable in introducing a greater balance between the emphasis on new life in Christ and the remission of sin. Previously, when the rite was largely private in observance and punctiliar in nature, the forgiveness of sin (and in particular, original sin, as understood in the Western Christian tradition) was the principal focus of baptism. In this rebalancing, the priority of "new life" in, with, and through Christ is established. And, not to put too fine a point on it, the consequent "remission of sins" for those incorporated into the body of Christ, stands out as *crucial* in the Baptismal Rite.

Yet even from the earliest times, the Church has struggled to maintain this balance and priority. The tension can especially be seen in the chronological unease with which the Evangelists deal with the questions around the baptism of Jesus. While all the Evangelists emphasize Jesus anointing by the Spirit, taking them in chronological order, after Mark's original account of Jesus's baptism (Mark 1:9–11), the other Evangelists are increasingly uneasy about Jesus undergoing John's baptism for the remission of sins (see Matt. 3:13–17; Luke 3:21–22). By the time of John's Gospel, Jesus is not baptized at all, but rather is twice proclaimed by the Baptist as the Christ, the "Lamb of God who takes away the sin of the world"

(John 1:29–39). So the problem of priority about sins vs new life has been there from the beginning. Perhaps the best contemporary resolution of the difficulty is George Timms's "The sinless One to Jordan came" (*The Hymnal 1982*, # 120).

Even so, it is important for the Church now in this post-Christendom age to assert the priority of "new life" in Christ as exactly the ground for the "remission of sin" and not the other way around, thus making forgiveness a precondition for that "new life."

There is a particular point in the 1979 baptismal liturgy that would benefit from a revision of language to reflect this theological rebalancing and priority. It comes in the first sentence introducing the Prayer for the Gifts of the Spirit as it appears between the actions of the water rite and the chrismation of the baptized. That sentence might reverse the order of the images used:

> Heavenly Father, we thank you that by water and the Holy Spirit you have bestowed upon *these* your *servants* the forgiveness of sin, and have raised *them* to the new life of grace. (BCP, 308)

to become:

> Heavenly Father, we thank you that by water and the Holy Spirit you have raised *these* your *servants* to the new life of grace, thereby bestowing upon *them* the forgiveness of sin.

2. Renunciation & Affirmation Language

Among the calls for further revision of the Baptismal Rite, some voices have addressed the multifaceted subject of language. Suggestions have ranged along a wide spectrum. A common factor, however, appears to be a desire for a more robust and contemporary language at certain significant points in the rite. In this regard, the language of the threefold renunciations and affirmations (BCP, 302–3) have come under scrutiny. The third question in the renunciations reads:

> Do you renounce all sinful desires that draw you from the love of God?

It is the phrase "all sinful desires" that presents the problem in several respects. A preliminary problem with the whole phrase revolves around what most people in contemporary culture will imagine when they hear these words, namely, that an analysis of sin is exhausted by reference to sexual temptations or the yielding to them. A more profound understanding of sin, however, reveals that lust is only the tip of the iceberg that threatens shipwreck for human flourishing and fulfillment as intended by God. (Dante, in his *Divine Comedy*, puts lust as the last sinful disposition to be reformed, holding the other deadly six as of far greater consequence.)

Secondarily, if the words "sinful desires" are stressed, the preceding word "all" might imply that there are some sinful desires that do not draw us from the love of God—this, of course, is a *reductio ad absurdum*. A similar resulting implication can occur if the word "sinful" alone is stressed. But the major difficulty here from a theological standpoint is the conjunction of these words with "desires" and the implication that this word is by association with "sinful" somehow tainted in itself.

It is, however, the case—at least from a Christian perspective—that human beings are primarily *desiring* beings. This in no way denigrates the compliment we give ourselves in calling humankind *homo sapiens*—we would not know ourselves to be principally desiring creatures without the thinking function (intellect) that enables us to reflect upon experience as well as to articulate and communicate the result of such reflection. These are modern expressions of a tradition in Christian theology that goes at least as far back as St. Augustine (if not to scripture) and which were given splendid imaginative exhibition in Dante's *Divine Comedy* along the way. There we discover that love (desire) is at the root of every admirable virtue as well as all culpable vice (sin). The human problem is at root, then, not desire, but disordered desires. Put another way in relation to baptism, our new life in Christ—both individually and as community—offers the possibility of the right ordering of our desires with regard to self, others, and God. It also offers the release from the habitual distortion of desire, that is, the misdirections, defections, and excesses of desire which, collectively, constitute sin.

Bringing these points to bear on the issue at hand, then, what alternative language can be suggested for the third renunciation in the Baptismal Rite? A possible straightforward query might be:

> Do you renounce deforming sin that draws you from the love of God?

The multiple and protean deformations of a human nature created good by God, but subject to distortion and damnable results for the soul and the human community in general, are better set forth by the comprehensive phrase "deforming sin" rather than "all sinful desires." A major confusion is avoided and a more adequate anatomy of sin and its seriousness is exhibited as it deserves to be renounced.

3. Placement of the Baptismal Covenant

A proposal to place the Apostles' Creed closer to the baptism and marking with oil has already been cogently made by Bishop Neil Alexander and other liturgical theologians. The ancient creed of the Western Catholic Church in the rite's question-and-response form serves to set forth the Baptismal Covenant. It does this not only in our affirmation of who is the God we worship (in contradistinction from other possible gods), but also by specifically indicating what God in "Trinity of Persons and Unity of Being" *has* done, *is* doing, and *will* bring to completion "for us and for our salvation."

The repositioning of the Baptismal Covenant as setting forth our affirmation of a promise from which such a God will never default deserves to be placed just prior to the baptismal action that effects it.

4. Seeing & Hearing Water Poured

Outstanding among the enrichments of the 1979 BCP's Baptismal Rite is the comprehensive "Thanksgiving over the Water" (pp. 306–7). It is a model blessing that consecrates a thing by giving thanks for it and opens up or reveals its inherent goodness and use through God's creation. Given, then, this abundant prayer of blessing and the singular importance of water at baptism, we wish to offer a suggestion. The appended "Additional Directions" for the rite reads: "Where practicable, the font is to be filled with clean water immediately before the Thanksgiving over the Water" (BCP, 313). For the congregation and those being baptized this is both a visible and audible ceremonial direction in regard to the water. The following alternative direction is proposed to further enhance the significance of the action:

> *As the Thanksgiving over the Water is sung or said, the Deacon or other appointed person pours water from a suitable ewer into the font initially at the end of the sentence referencing Creation; then again after the sentence referencing the Exodus; and finally after the sentence regarding Jesus as the Christ.*

This suggested alteration has several advantages. First, it provides for the statement of a norm in suggesting the priority of singing to saying. Second, the three-fold action of pouring water at specific moments during the Thanksgiving gives further emphasis to the sign of water. And, finally, giving this action appropriately into the hands of the deacon or other appointed person, frees the presiding priest or bishop to concentrate on the performance of the blessing itself.

5. *Prayer for the Gifts of the Spirit*

The Baptismal Rite places the Prayer for the Seven Gifts of the Spirit directly between the water baptism and the marking with oil. There is, however, a note following this sealing by the Holy Spirit that allows for the Gifts prayer to be said *after* that action:

> *Or this action may be done immediately after the administration of the water and before the preceding prayer.* (BCP, 308)

We have earlier underscored the direct association of the Holy Spirit as the anointing or confirming of Jesus as the Christ at his baptism. And it is precisely the seven gifts of the Spirit, so effectively translated in the 1979 rite, that are enumerated in Christian tradition by reference to Isaiah 11:1–3, "A shoot shall come out from the stump of Jesse . . . and the spirit of the Lord shall rest on him"—following which the gifts are specified. One of the brilliant features of their translation in the 1979 rite is the gifts as sustaining and energizing dispositions invoked for the new life of the baptized: *inquiring* for wisdom, *discerning* for understanding, *to persevere* for ghostly strength, and so on. But perhaps best of all the gift of "joy and wonder," which is a more positive nuancing of "holy fear."

It is exactly these defining Christ-like gifts that are invoked upon those newly baptized into the body of Christ, so that we may then complete the action by declaring to them "You are sealed by the Holy Spirit" and marking them with the character, the cross, of Christ. To do otherwise with the placement of the Prayer for the Gifts of the Spirit would serve only to denigrate the Spirit's work by making it appear as an afterthought to the baptismal action.

6. Repositioning the Covenantal Promises

At the conclusion of Section 3 above, we noted that a further refinement to placing the covenant closer to the baptismal action could be made. In one of the most significant aspects of the 1979 Baptismal Rite, a series of behavioral promises was conjoined to the question-and-response form of the Apostles' Creed. These responsive promises make explicit the empowering and ethical requisites of new life in the body of Christ that are, in fact, the implications of lifelong baptismal living. Communally considered, these aspects of the covenant represent essential dimensions of the reign of God / kingdom of Christ / commonwealth of the Holy Spirit as well.

The difficulty in their present placement as appended to the Apostles' Creed has to do with the manner of mediating God's grace. The creedal portion of the Baptismal Covenant represents God's initiative "for us and for our salvation." To append our promises as the human response to God's grace at this point prior to the baptismal action at the very least implies that our promises form a *condition* for receiving God's saving grace. Even the acknowledgment by us that we can fulfill those promises only "with God's help" (BCP, 304–5) is not sufficient to free them from the implication.

This taint of heresy can, however, be expunged by placing the human response promises of the covenant directly following the baptismal action in the rite. Yet a question remains as to whether this "splitting" of the covenant does not denigrate the divine-human unity of the covenant. A closer look at the effect of ritual pattern or structure in this case reveals not so much a division of the covenant, but rather, that the two aspects of the covenant so placed actually serve to *enfold* the baptismal action. And this action incorporating us into the body of Christ is precisely the mediation between heaven and earth, between God and humanity, that is celebrated in the Paschal Mystery: the covenant enfolding the action even as the action unifies the two aspects of the covenant.

7. Recipimus te!–Singing the Welcome

Revision here involves only the addition of one short bit of direction after the assembly is invited to welcome the newly baptized: the congregation then sings or says that welcome.

We have noted that a singularly important aspect of the 1979 Baptsmal Rite was its recovery of baptism as a public liturgy. It was further noticed that this reformation brought three parties together in covenant relationship: the Triune God; the candidates for baptism and their sponsors; and the congregation as the local incarnation of the church. The congregation stands out in this light in several ways, first as the faithful are themselves involved at every such liturgy in renewing their own vows, and secondly as they promise to be supportive of the newly baptized for their life in Christ (BCP, 292, 303). But even more than these important facets of congregational involvement is the welcome extended to the newly baptized as those assembled speak for the entire Church throughout the world. As the welcome into the household of God is extended, it is marked by two imperatives and an invitation:

> *[C]onfess* the faith of Christ crucified, *proclaim* his resurrection, and *share* with us in his eternal priesthood. (BCP, 308, emphasis added)

Perhaps no more succinct and powerful statement of the obligations and opportunities of new life in the body of Christ—overtly, liturgically acknowledged as the priesthood of all believers—as we live in and toward the fullness of the reign of God / kingdom of Christ / commonwealth of the Holy Spirit could be imagined. Such a moment deserves voices joyfully raised in song. In the face of such a proposal, we would be remiss if we did not conclude with a splendid example of such service music as presented on the next page.

Questions for Discussion

1. Part one of the chapter recommends expanding the preface to include a section entitled "Preparing for Baptism." Why is such an addition to the preface necessary to fulfilling the original intentions for the life and mission of the Episcopal Church as set forth in the BCP 1979 rite of Christian initiation?
2. The essay proposes that the two parts of the Baptismal Covenant enfold the water baptism-chrismation action. How does the dialogue form of the Apostles' Creed serve to articulate God's irrevocable part of the covenant? What is the effect in the rite's celebration of placing the baptized person(s) and the sponsor's promises after the water baptism-chrismation?
3. The author recommends that an optional placement of the Prayer for the Gifts of the Spirit be eliminated, ensuring that this prayer invariably occur between the water baptism and the chrismational action. Why does the invocation of these seven gifts (based on Isaiah 11:1–3) at this location form an essential part of the baptism-chrismation?

This music was composed by Carol A. Doran, DMA. With printed attribution, Dr. Doran has given permission for this music to be reproduced for congregational singing.

8
Baptism and Ordination in the BCP 1979

Elise A. Feyerherm

The whole creation is called into being through the abundant love of God, who in Christ participates in the world's life so that we may share in the triune life of love and joy. Through the Holy Spirit God baptizes us into the life and ministry of Christ and forms us into the laos, the people of God, who as signs and agents of God's reign participate in God's mission of reconciling humanity and all creation to God. This is the ecclesia, the church, the new community called into being by God. The foundation of the life and ministry of the church is therefore baptism.
—International Anglican Liturgical Consultation

AS EPISCOPALIANS, OUR understanding of the nature and structure of the church is based in and flows from the priesthood that belongs to all Christians through the gifts of the Holy Spirit bestowed in their baptism. The Episcopal Church's prayer book of 1979 is intended to reflect a "baptismal ecclesiology" which seeks to reveal and nourish this priesthood of all believers, in contrast to traditional hierarchical models of the church that view the church through the prism of its ordained leadership. If (or since) baptism (rather than ordination) is the ground of Christian ministry, then the rite of baptism is not the only place where we should expect such an understanding of the nature of the church to show up; we should see it in every sacrament and service within our prayer book, including (and perhaps especially) ordination.

As we lean into the call of the 79th General Convention to engage in the "ongoing work of liturgical and prayer book revision for the future of God's mission through the Episcopal branch of the Jesus movement," we discover that the rites of ordination have a great deal to tell us about where the Episcopal Church has been and where God is leading us. As with baptism, the language and shape of ordination rites both reflect and mold our understanding of what ministry is, who engages in it, and how the Church is organized within itself and for service to the world. Our liturgies for baptism and ordination need to be consistent with one another, speaking authentically of our experience of the Holy Spirit as well as of our evolving understanding of ministry. They also need to reflect our conviction that all the baptized share in ministry through the priesthood of believers and that authority in the Church is not scattered about willy-nilly, but must answer to the continuous apostolic tradition handed down to us over the centuries.

The Work of the Holy Spirit: Infusion or Release?

An important understanding within our tradition is that the Holy Spirit does really work in and through the church and its liturgies. All of the sacraments in the Episcopal Church have in common the invocation of the Holy Spirit (*epiclesis*). We ask the Spirit to come upon what we are blessing: in baptism, water; in the Eucharist, bread and wine, as well as the gathered assembly (a "double epiclesis"), and in ordination, the person who has been chosen and set apart for the ministry of a bishop, presbyter, or deacon. But how do we understand the work of the Holy Spirit in the sacraments? Is some supernatural substance being inserted? Is there what is called an "ontological" change in the water, bread, wine, or human being, meaning that there is an actually transformation of the very being of what is being blessed? Is the change more in our perception or our relationship to what is being blessed? Or is all of this happening at once? Our language is woefully inadequate when it comes to expressing what the Holy Spirit is doing in our midst, especially in the sacraments, but we are called to be as clear as we can, especially in our liturgy.

One way of understanding the blessing bestowed by the Spirit is to view it not so much as an infusion of some supernatural quality, but rather a *revealing* and *sanctifying* of the goodness that God has already created and bestowed. But the rites as we have them tend not to be as clear about this as they might. In baptism, the presider asks God to "sanctify this water, we pray you, by the power of your Holy Spirit" (BCP, 307). In the Eucharist, the request is for the Holy Spirit to "sanctify" (Prayers A and C); "send your Holy Spirit upon these gifts" (Prayer B); and in Prayer D, that the Holy Spirit may "descend" upon us and upon the gifts of bread and wine. All of these invocations could be interpreted to mean that when the Holy Spirit descends (and then departs?), something is there that wasn't there before.

We could say the same thing about the rite of ordination. When a priest or deacon is ordained, the bishop asks God the Father to "give your Holy Spirit to N.; fill [*her/him/them*] with grace and power, and make [*her/him/them*] a [*priest/deacon*] in your Church" (BCP, 533, 545). The invocation of the Spirit in the ordination of a bishop is more elaborate, not only requesting that "the power of your princely Spirit" be poured out upon the candidate, but also identifying this princely Spirit with Jesus Christ and the apostles, thus locating the newly ordained bishop within the direct line of apostolic succession (BCP, 521).

This kind of language suggests that the Holy Spirit puts something in the person being ordained that was not there before, just as in baptism the language seems to suggest that the water and the person being baptized are receiving some kind of new substance. But is this really what we believe is happening? Or, if we do believe that something substantive is being given, is it some indelible, ontological change in the person being ordained or the release of a gift or calling to be used on behalf of the Church? This is the fundamental question to be asked of both baptism and ordination: in these two deeply connected sacraments, what is the Holy Spirit actually doing?

In the case of baptism, God has already created this person in the image of God, complete with gifts for the nourishing and renewal of the world; the Holy Spirit acts not to infuse but to release and sanctify this person and their gifts for the work of healing creation in God's name. The prayer immediately following baptism tells us even more about what the church believes is happening: in this prayer, the presider gives thanks for the work of the Holy Spirit in forgiving sin and raising the newly baptized to "the new life of grace." The language is more about bringing God-given gifts to fruition, human qualities of curiosity and discernment, courage, agency, and perseverance, and especially gifts of love, joy, and wonder (BCP, 308). These are not just Christian qualities; they are profoundly human ones. In baptism, the Holy Spirit works to enliven the divine image in which every human being has been created.

In the case of ordination, the Holy Spirit is also working to enliven the divine image within the person being ordained. The Spirit is called to come upon a person whose gifts have already been recognized through the long process of preparation for ordination; these gifts are not implanted so much as they are released and sustained for the good of the whole church and the world. As the bishop lays hands on the person to be ordained, the bishop prays on behalf of the gathered community, and indeed the whole Church: "Therefore, Father, through Jesus Christ your Son, give your Holy Spirit to N.; fill *her* with grace and power, and make *her* a priest in your Church" (BCP, 533). The work of the Holy Spirit in this instance (as always and in every instance) is to make the person being ordained who she really, deeply, already is. This is in keeping with what we understand to be happening in baptism.

The language of "making" someone a priest, however, is a bit of a sticking point; it is not exactly what we mean to say. In baptism, this person is already a priest sharing in the priesthood of Jesus Christ; we know this from the baptism rite itself, as the gathered assembly welcomes the newly baptized into the household of God. So what exactly do we mean when the bishop prays to *make* someone a priest? It is helpful to think in the terms already mentioned, that the one being ordained is being made not something other than she already is, but more deeply herself. But in that case, why do we need ordination? Doesn't baptism do that already? One way of understanding the difference is that ordination makes someone a priest specifically in—and for—the church, while baptism makes someone a priest in and for the world outside the church. How these priesthoods are related is a key issue, and has everything to do with why and how we ordain.

Who Is a Priest? Believers, Bishops, Presbyters, and Deacons

Baptism and ordination are both rites that speak to our understanding of Christian priesthood. Although it has become commonplace to use the term "priest" only in reference to someone who is ordained to preach and preside at the sacraments, the rite of baptism makes it clear that a particular kind of priesthood belongs to all the baptized by virtue of our union with Christ. In the 1979 prayer book, the assembly welcomes the newly baptized with these words: "We receive you into the household of God. Confess the faith of Christ crucified, proclaim his resurrection, and share with us in his eternal priesthood" (BCP, 308). What is this priesthood that all Christians share through their baptism? A priest is someone who stands between God and the world, offering up the needs of the world to God, and communicating the blessings of their particular experience of God to the world. As L. William Countryman has written in *Living on the Border of the Holy*, all humans share in this priestly calling on some level, whatever their religious beliefs and practices; all the baptized share in a particular version of this calling that is modeled on and originates in Jesus Christ. When we invite the newly baptized to share in Christ's eternal priesthood, it is this "priesthood of all believers" that is being signified, though the meaning of the words often bypasses us in the moment.

Since baptism initiates a person into priesthood, in the sense that all members of the body of Christ mediate Christ in the world, we need to be clear about what ordination is and how it connects to this basic priesthood. Ordination, whether of a bishop, priest, or deacon, points to a *particular* form of ministry with a particular role to play in the order and governance of the Church. Those who are ordained live out their baptismal priesthood by building up the body of Christ and empowering others to enact their own priesthood: "In order that the whole people of God may fulfill their calling to be a holy priesthood, serving the world by ministering Christ's reconciling love in the power of the Spirit, some are called to specific ministries of leadership by ordination" ("To Equip the Saints" 2001).

The liturgies of ordination in the prayer book reflect this particular role of the ordained. All liturgies of ordination are in the context of the Holy Eucharist, which locates ordained ministry within the mission of the whole people of God. In the ordination rite itself, the Examination in each case articulates clearly how the ordained person will be called to equip the people of God. Bishops are reminded that they are "to be in all things a faithful pastor and wholesome example for the entire flock of Christ" (BCP, 517). Priests are to "nourish Christ's people from the riches of his grace, and strengthen them to glorify God in this life and in the life to come," (BCP, 531) and deacons "are to show Christ's people that in serving the helpless they are serving Christ himself" (BCP, 543).

Within the Church, bishops are called to the ministry of oversight, visible signs of the unity and apostolic roots of our faith; presbyters are called to preach, teach, preside at the sacraments, and provide pastoral care; deacons are called to engage the body of Christ more fully in its work of addressing the needs of the world. These are particular roles within the church that have to do with organization, governance, mission, and spiritual nourishment, without which the gathered community might lack focus, coherence, direction, and endurance. As Louis Weil points out, ordination involves much more than a particular role in the liturgy; the ordained person's liturgical function is a sign of "a specific gift for pastoral oversight" in some way. It is a reflection of a more comprehensive relationship with the gathered community, one that extends well beyond the celebration of the Eucharist and takes root in the actual life and ministry of the Christian community to which the ordained person is called.

So ordination does set a person apart to do specific things in and for the body of Christ. And those who are ordained also, because of their vows, accept greater responsibility, especially for keeping the church connected to the tradition that has been handed down to us from Jesus through the apostles. In this way, bishops, priests, and deacons have a certain amount of authority in the church, by virtue of the community's recognition of their gifts for leadership, and by what they are called to do. But two things especially need to be emphasized here: 1) those who are ordained do not suddenly lose their essential baptismal priesthood of serving the rest of the world when hands are laid on them, and 2) the priesthoods of lay and ordained are not ranked. One is not more important than the other.

Ordination does not replace baptism; it simply focuses it in a particular way. The term "laity" comes from *laos*, which means "people"—bishops, priests, and deacons are still part of the people, only with a particular, and sacred, role. In many ways, our current ordination rites visibly reflect the Episcopal Church's testimony that priesthood belongs to all the baptized and that ordination in no way supplants this most basic priesthood. Laypersons participate more visibly than they once did in the ordination rites themselves, presenting and vesting the candidates, and serving in liturgical roles as litanists, readers, and intercessors. Candidates for ordination currently enter the church in a simple white alb, a sign of baptism, without any marker of the order to which they will be ordained. First and foremost, they are baptized into Christ, along with the whole people of God in the Church.

The call to ordination also does not increase the status of one's baptismal priesthood, but rather recognizes those who are to be ordained as those who are "called by God and discerned by the body to be signs and animators of Christ's self-giving life and ministry to which all people are called" ("To Equip the Saints" 2001). To be a "sign and animator" is to focus one's ordained ministry on empowering others, following Jesus's teaching that "whoever wishes to be great among you must be your servant, and whoever wishes to be first among you must be your slave; just as the Son of Man came not to be served but to serve, and to give his life a ransom for many" (Matt. 20:26–28).

It has been pointed out by many, however, that ordinations still possess a whiff of being "coronations," focusing too much on those being ordained and not enough on the specific connections between ordained and lay ministry. While baptisms generally take place on Sunday mornings, in the context of a parish Eucharist, ordinations are highly choreographed events outside of Sunday morning, often involving months of planning. My sense is that we approach baptisms much more casually, inserting the baptismal rite into our usual Sunday morning liturgy and adding the occasional baptismal hymn, but not much more. Over the millennia those who have planned and led liturgies have tended to infuse a great deal more pageantry and emotional weight into ordinations, in large part because we have a hard time shedding the "mystique of spiritual sacerdotal power," as Mary Collins phrases it (Collins 1983).

One question has to do with the terminology we use for ordained ministries; in particular, that of a priest. Over the centuries, this has been a question fraught with angst; until fairly recently, Anglican prayer books have generally identified the ordained person who presides at the sacraments and has pastoral oversight of a congregation as a "minister." The term "priest" only entered the American prayer book in 1928, reflecting a greater respect for the catholic roots of the Anglican tradition and reverence for our sacramental tradition. But we have to admit that the waters are definitely muddied when we use the term "priesthood" in reference to both the ordained and the laity. The term "presbyter" (meaning *elder*) could be used instead of "minister" or "priest"—this is historically and linguistically more accurate. This option, however, muddies different waters, potentially leading some to confuse our tradition with those in the Reformed tradition that go by the name "Presbyterian." Language being the rich and ambiguous tool that it is, this is not an easy question.

Another way of reinforcing the centrality of baptism to ordination is to include in every ordination the reaffirmation of the Baptismal

Covenant, either as part of the gathering rite or after the liturgy of the Word. Imagine an ordination in which all who are gathered have an opportunity to proclaim once again their own call to the priesthood of the baptized; how would this change our experience of ordination if it were made more clear that the Baptismal Covenant is the heart of why we are ordaining people in the first place? Another possibility is to end the liturgy with the promises of the Baptismal Covenant, as a kind of commissioning of both laity and ordained. Positioned immediately before the dismissal by the deacon, these promises would remind all those present of the nature of our common priesthood and the very purpose for which we are being sent from Christ's table into the world.

As we consider revising our ordination liturgies, we need to think about ways to resist its mystique without, of course, undermining the significance of ordained ministry. So how might we more clearly lift up in our ordination liturgies the baptismal roots of ministry and the fundamental equality of the whole people of God? One way is to continue to emphasize the interconnectedness of all four orders of Christian ministry by ensuring that all four have a visible role to play in the ordination liturgy: the episcopate (bishops), the presbyterate (priests), the diaconate (deacons), and the laity (all the baptized).

Other Anglican provinces have been thinking about this very question; the prayer book of New Zealand, for instance, gives the laity an actual speaking role in the ordination prayer, a prayer that has traditionally belonged solely to the bishop. In each of the ordination services, for bishop, priest, and deacon, the gathered assembly adds its assent not only with a simple "Amen," but with a short prayer that echoes the particular role which the ordained person will take on in the community (*A New Zealand Prayer Book* 1988, 897, 908, 921). In liturgy and in our common life, the bishop has been given the authority to speak on behalf of the whole community; there are, however, times when it is important to give the laity a more explicit voice, especially when a leader is being set apart for ministry. Our own liturgies of ordination could easily do something similar to what the New Zealand prayer book has done, drawing out the essential role that the whole Church plays in the act of ordination.

The church as a whole serves the world in Christ's name; those who are ordained serve the world, certainly, but their liturgical roles bear witness to (and are an integral part of) the special responsibility they have to minister to, encourage, and empower all the baptized in ministering to the world. As we continue to use the 1979 prayer book, and as we look toward a new incarnation of our prayer book in the future, we will need to examine our rites of baptism and ordination alike for their clarity not only around each order of ministry, but also how this diversified yet coherent mission to the world is carried out.

Together, baptism and ordination reflect God's call to the church to serve and heal the world in Christ's name, and the work of the Holy Spirit in nourishing and sustaining that call. Baptism brings people into this sacred vocation; ordination serves to order the body that it may more faithfully witness to the world in the name of the Triune God. What we cannot forget is that baptism is the root of ordination and not the other way around, and that it is the Holy Spirit that flows through it all, that we may "confess the faith of Christ crucified, proclaim his resurrection, and share . . . in his eternal priesthood" (BCP, 308).

Questions for Discussion

1. Have you ever attended an ordination? What aspects of the liturgy reinforced the connection between ordination and baptism? What aspects undermined that connection?
2. What does the priesthood of all believers mean to you?
3. The scholar and priest Louis Weil has said that as the Church, "We baptize priests; we ordain presbyters [elders]." What is the continuity as well as the difference between the priesthood of all believers and the priesthood of the elders whom we call priests?
4. How might our liturgy of baptism better highlight the dignity and authenticity of the priesthood of all believers?
5. How might our liturgy of ordination better express the fundamental connection between baptism and ordination?

9

On the Integrity of Eucharistic Communion

Louis Weil

IN THE OPENING document of the 1979 Book of Common Prayer, "Concerning the Service of the Church," the first sentence makes an affirmation grounded in the ancient tradition of the Church: it affirms that the Holy Eucharist is "the principal act of Christian worship on the Lord's Day. . ." (BCP, 13).

The significance of this phrase, reclaiming as it does the centrality of the Eucharist in the life of the Church, has often been noted, but its full implications have been obscured in the Church's liturgical practice. The phrase quoted above refers to "the Holy Eucharist" and not to "the Holy Communion" as the central act of Christian worship. Since the reception of the consecrated gifts is an integral part of the rite, it may seem that this is a false distinction, but it is in fact an essential distinction. "Holy Eucharist" refers to the entire rite. "Holy Communion" refers to the reception of the bread and wine that have been consecrated in the proclamation of the Great Thanksgiving *at that celebration of the Eucharist.* The first term always refers to the entire rite; the second term may be used to refer to the entire rite but its primary meaning is a reference to the consecrated gifts that the people receive in communion. If for some pastoral reason the act of communion is separated from its integral place within the whole, a path is opened that may risk undermining fundamental aspects of Christian theology with regard to the Eucharist in the life of the Church, since by its nature communion is never a private act.

It is in the light of this risk that we must interpret the fifth resolution in the General Convention's "Plan for the Revision of the Book of Common Prayer" [A068]. It reads: "That this church continue to engage the deep Baptismal and Eucharistic theology and practice of the 1979 Prayer Book." The document thus reminds us that development continues in the life of the church, including the forms of its public worship. The shared experience of common prayer embodies our common faith, so that any major revision becomes a serious undertaking on the part of all the church's members. The often-repeated sharing of familiar forms of prayer plays a fundamental role in the nourishment of the common faith of those who pray—and that experience is of the eucharistic rite in its entirety.

Then what of communion on other occasions, when it is given outside the context of the entire rite? The underlying norm that is the foundation of the statement that "The Holy Eucharist is the principal act of Christian worship on the Lord's Day" is that the entire eucharistic action, *all of the constitutive elements which together form the rite,* must be understood in their complementary integrity. Pastoral exceptions, although occasionally required by particular pastoral needs such as the bringing of communion to the sick, should never undermine the essential unity of those elements that *together* embody the "norm."

The practice of carrying the eucharistic bread and wine to those members of the community who were unable to be present at the Sunday assembly arose very early in the Church's life. The conviction that all the baptized should receive communion each Sunday was an important expression of Christian identity. If the elements could not be taken directly from the liturgy, there was a practical need that they be stored until they were taken to the communicant.

Very gradually various containers were designed which offered a distinct place for that purpose. A discussion of the development of such containers would carry us beyond the focus of this chapter. Let it suffice here for us to note that such "reservation" originated for very practical reasons, essentially so that communion would be available according to pastoral need. The place where the elements were thus "reserved" very gradually became a place to be honored, perhaps with prayer or perhaps with a gesture such as a bow. But what is most significant is that the primary purpose for this putting aside of some of the consecrated elements was that they might be available for the communion of people who could not attend the celebration of the Eucharist. That purpose for reservation has continued to the present time, but once put aside for this purpose, the consecrated elements embody both the presence of Christ in the gifts, but also the relation of the sick person to their parish community.

The earliest practice of the Church with regard to the reception of communion was always with elements consecrated *at that Eucharist.* Members of the congregation who might be sick and unable to attend the Eucharist with their community were fed by the church's ministers as a pastoral extension of the communion of those assembled. The elements were not reserved for those who were present at the assembly, but for those who were absent. In the eucharistic action, communion is shared with those who have gathered for the particular celebration. At the same time, this act is our communion with all the members of the body of the Risen Lord—*all members,* living and departed, who together with us form the one Mystical Body of Christ. The integrity of that eucharistic action requires the normative practice that all who have gathered receive the consecrated gifts which embody the oblation of the people in that celebration.

By the late sixth and early seventh centuries, however, communion of the laity had begun a precipitous decline. There was no textual emphasis on the term "communion" since, as the patterns of eucharistic worship developed, the emphasis in practice was upon the communion of the priest/celebrant. By the late Middle Ages, the focus for the laity in the Mass ritual was upon the elevation of the host, that is, the lifting up of the bread that would then be consumed as the communion of the priest, during the Eucharistic

Prayer. Eucharistic Communion of the congregation had become a "piety of vision" rather than a "piety of reception," and writers defended the spiritual value of "ocular communion." The reception of the consecrated bread and wine in the communion of the laity had become so infrequent that by the time of the Fourth Lateran Council in 1215, a canon required that the laity receive the consecrated bread only once each year. A custom emerged that this annual reception should take place at Easter. The laity had come to be understood not as integral members of the eucharistic assembly, but rather as pious observers of the priest's actions. The words of the prayers were by that time deemed so sacred that they should not even be audible to the laity.

What does it mean for the laity to be "integral members of the eucharistic assembly"? During my half-century as a priest of the Church, I have often attended celebrations of the eucharistic rite at which I was neither the presider nor what is sometimes called "a concelebrant," but rather a member of the congregation, attentive to the needs of my elderly mother. It was in that context that I had extensive experience of the diverse ways in which my being a member of the assembly was understood. These ranged at one extreme in which the role of the laity was little more than saying an occasional response such as "And with thy spirit," to, at the other extreme, a parish in which the entire congregation recited the Eucharistic Prayer together, very much as a choral reading.

The contrast between these two models of active participation is clearly significant in that they demonstrate conflicting understandings of the role of baptized Christians in worship. Yet in both these situations, it must be noted, the reception of the consecrated bread and wine by the lay members was the unquestioned norm. A major achievement of Archbishop Thomas Cranmer in the first Book of Common Prayer (1549) was that the reception of communion by the laity should be integral at all celebrations of the Eucharist, and that has remained normative in Anglican practice ever since.

Our focus here is upon the integral role of reception of the consecrated gifts in communion. There are, however, liturgical contexts in which the integral role of communion as a shared action of the entire assembly has been set aside for legitimate pastoral reasons, such as for the communion of sick persons. Yet in this ministry as well the relation to the sharing of communion by the members of the parish has sometimes been obscured.

The most familiar context in which communion is given apart from the entire eucharistic action is in the Church's ministry to the sick, when either a member of the clergy or an appointed lay member of the congregation carries the elements to one who, because of sickness, is unable to participate in the Sunday morning assembly. Increasingly this ministry has expanded to include people whose age or health have created a situation in which they may never be physically able now or in the future to take their place in the Sunday assembly.

With regard to the reception of communion, how is their membership within the body of Christ to find a tangible embodiment? The communion of a sick person should never be understood as a "private communion." Rather it must take a form in which their membership in the parish is reaffirmed through the pattern in which that communion is administered. Although communion may be administered in the privacy of a hospital room or in the person's home, it is an extension of the shared communion of the gathered people at the parish church. Normally it is from that congregation that the elements have been carried forth to the sick person.

In my own ministry to the sick over these many years, my practice was, except in cases of severe illness, to offer the communion elements within a wider liturgical context in which one or more of the appointed Sunday scripture readings would be read by a layperson whom I would invite to assist me in this ministry. In this way, the sick person experienced this ministry as an action of the Church and not only of an ordained person. The assistance of a layperson was not always possible, but it happened often enough that the laity of the parish were aware that this was *our ministry* as a community of faith and not merely a private action of the priest. It also made a tangible connection with the naming of sick persons in the Prayers of the People at celebrations of the Eucharist in the parish.

Poor pastoral choices, however, can undermine the integrity of that relationship with the congregation. I can speak to this from a painful personal experience. Several months ago, I had an extended period of serious illness during which time I was unable to attend the Eucharist in my home parish. Communion was brought to me by a priest with long pastoral experience, and so it was that what unfolded during his visit surprised me. I do not question that the bread and wine brought to me that day had been duly consecrated, but in every other respect, especially with regard to the relationship of the elements to the Eucharist celebrated by my parish community, the essential signification was seriously impaired.

The visit was scheduled about an hour after a weekday celebration in a nearby parish, rather than on a Sunday afternoon. I recognized the small black case in which the elements were carried, and I presumed that they had been consecrated at the Eucharist that day. When the case was opened, however, and the priest came to my bedside to give me communion, what was given to me to eat was more akin to cardboard than to bread. When I drank from the small chalice, the wine was bitterly sour.

By an act of faith, I received them as the body and blood of Christ, but they had not been consecrated that day nor the previous Sunday. It was impossible to know how many weeks or even months earlier my communion had been consecrated at a celebration of the Eucharist at which members of the people of God had been present. My point is that what I was given that day embodied no tangible relationship to the community of which I was a member and with whom I regularly shared the eucharistic elements. Quite apart from their staleness and sourness, the elements had become "holy objects" rather than spiritual food. In a sense, they were "talismans" of the body and blood of Christ rather than the sacred food that would embody my membership in a living community and thus instruments by which my membership in my community of faith was nourished and sustained. I experienced no tangible association with that community.

This is perhaps an extreme example, but during the course of my illness what I have described happened three times, administered to me by different priests who were perhaps not fully aware of what had happened to the two elements as they were stored for many weeks or months in the tabernacle. How had we arrived at a point where the consecrated elements reserved for the communion of the sick could become so separated from the communion of the people gathered that day or the previous Sunday in our home parish? The bread and wine as sacred objects had become detached from the community and context in which they had been consecrated.

When we compare this pattern with the ancient tradition of the carrying of the consecrated elements immediately from a celebration of the Eucharist to Christians who could not be present because they were imprisoned in preparation for their martyrdom, or to the sick for whom only their illness could keep them from being present in the assembly, we begin to see what has been lost when that bridge with the living community has been obscured. This essential connection is still seen centuries later in the preparation of the first Book of Common Prayer by Archbishop Thomas Cranmer. There we find that the rubrical directions indicate that the normal practice was to carry the elements to the sick person directly from a celebration of the Eucharist at which, apart from illness, the sick person would have been present.

It is difficult to explain how this development occurred, but I would suggest that at least in part the explanation is an unintended byproduct of a major concern of the leaders of the Oxford Movement of the nineteenth century. Under the impact of the Enlightenment, some English church leaders had so emphasized a rational perspective to Christian doctrine that the supernatural aspects of Christian faith were obscured or rejected. This, of course, had particular impact upon the understanding of the sacraments. How could a "rational faith" affirm the Real Presence of Christ in the consecrated elements when our eyes told us that they remained merely bread and wine? Under the impact of rational criteria, by the beginning of the nineteenth century, sacramental worship had all but disappeared from the normal experience of the English Christians who took the trouble to go to church. If they did attend, it was often to hear something more like a lecture on moral values than to participate in an act of sacramental worship.

One of the main achievements of the Oxford Movement was the recovery and renewal of sacramental life and practice in the English Church, most notably in its emphasis on the central place of the Eucharist in the Christian life. This recovery was theological as well as pastoral in that it fostered the ancient teaching that Christ is truly present in the Eucharist, which is not merely a remembrance of what Christ did long ago. This led gradually to a particular focus upon Christ's presence in the eucharistic gifts. In their desire to recover a sure foundation for their teaching, the Oxford leaders had, in general, turned to late medieval theology, which under the impact of the Romantic Movement of the nineteenth century viewed the High Middle Ages as the great period of Christian faith. The loss of active lay participation which we noted earlier is, however, but one sign that this turning to medieval theology may have been well-intentioned but inadequate for authentic eucharistic renewal. This had become a key issue at the time of the Reformation in the sixteenth century, and continued as a divisive issue among the various Christian traditions well into the twentieth century. This was as true of the English church as of the other Reformation churches. The intense focus on Christ's presence in the consecrated elements carried over from medieval teaching into the theology of the Oxford theologians.

The recovery of the full scope of Christ's presence in the Eucharist was left to theologians of the twentieth century. A major contribution to this recovery was achieved by the Roman Catholic bishops at the Second Vatican Council. The first document issued by the Council was the Constitution on the Sacred Liturgy (*Sacrosanctum Concilium* 1963).

In the seventh paragraph of that document, the text affirms the various modes in which Christ is present in the Eucharist. The document thus cut through the unending debates between Catholics and Protestants as to the nature of "the Real Presence." Those debates had produced a polarization between the various Christian traditions which ranged between the affirmation of a literal physical presence and, at the other extreme, a "memorialism" that in effect saw the Eucharist as a mere remembrance of Christ.

The document places the question of Christ's presence in the eucharistic action as a whole: it is found first in the gathering of the Christian people for the celebration "where two or three are gathered together in my name." Christ is then also found to be present in the proclamation of the Word; in the sacramental actions and prayers of the people; in the ministry of the priest; and in the consecrated eucharistic gifts. It is this theology of Christ's presence through a holistic understanding of the "eucharistic action" that underlies our focus here on the integrity of eucharistic communion.

At least in part, this may explain how an emphasis on the objective Presence in the consecrated elements might contribute to an unhelpful distinction in which the consecrated elements set apart for the communion of the sick might obscure the essential bridge between the consecrated elements and the gathered assembly among whom the bread and wine were consecrated. This might have contributed to a loss of the significant connection between the Eucharist of the assembly and the taking of communion to the sick. However this happened, it eroded a dimension of basic eucharistic theology which understands the Eucharist and communion within the context of the Church as body of Christ, and not merely as an act of personal and private piety.

We must acknowledge that problems have arisen in the past which we now see to have been aberrations in which the integrity of eucharistic celebrations was undermined. Perhaps the most significant example is the centuries during which the communion of the laity virtually disappeared. Liturgical historians have noted that in the ninth century there was a change in the Christian understanding of "the holy"—for something to be "holy" it had to be unlike the ordinary. The impact of this idea upon the pattern of eucharistic celebration was enormous. Several cultural and social factors contributed to the change. It was during this period that the eucharistic banquet became a sacred meal at which usually only the priest received communion. The laity had come to understand themselves as having no essential participatory role in communion. The reception of the consecrated elements at the eucharistic meal had ceased to embody the profound human experience of a shared meal.

In our own time, a utilitarian mindset has also undermined the authenticity of the meal character of the Eucharist. This development has been explored in depth in recent decades; the late Robert Taft, SJ, wrote about the loss of what he calls "a sharing of something we have and receive in common from God and share with one another—in short, a *communion.*" In this loss, there lies the risk that the common sense of the Eucharist will be obscured by an undermining of the integrity of the act of communion. The essential symbolic action of the Eucharist requires the common sharing of a common meal. Utilitarian priorities have no place in this: the integrity of the Eucharist is at stake. If the Holy Eucharist is, as the 1979 BCP claims, "the central act of Christian worship," that integrity must be held as a primary aspect of our stewardship of the sacramental life of the Church.

Questions for Discussion

1. Have you ever received communion during a time of illness, either in your home, or while in the hospital? If so, how would you speak of the difference between the more normative experience of communion at your parish church on a Sunday and on other related times?
2. The word "communion" suggests a sharing, namely the sharing of the consecrated bread and wine with others who together with you form the Sunday assembly of Christians. How do you experience this "sharing" as something which is essentially corporate—as something which Christians do together on the basis of a shared faith?
3. What are the diverse ways in which Christ is present in the Eucharist? How is each complementary of the others?
4. At a celebration of the Eucharist, do you expect that there will be a link between the reading of scripture and the sermon with the congregation's reception of the eucharistic gifts in communion? If so, how is this normally accomplished?

5. Saint Augustine taught that the Eucharist is "the Word made visible." This implies a significant connection between the proclamation of the Word in scripture and sermon with the sharing of the eucharistic gifts by the gathered community. Discuss the integral place of the proclamation of the Word of God and communion in the building up of the community of faith.

10

What Episcopalians Can Learn from Our Lutheran Communion Partners

about the Composition of Eucharistic Prayers

James Farwell

THE FRUITS OF the modern ecumenical movement are many. Not least among them is the capacity to learn from one another about the highest form of Christian practice: our worship. This is particularly true of what Episcopalians could learn about eucharistic praying from our full communion partners, the Evangelical Lutheran Church in America (ELCA).

The eucharistic prayers for use in the ELCA are among the most evocative, provocative, and beautiful offerings of thanksgiving to God currently in use among the churches of the Reformation. But why do eucharistic prayers matter anyway?

As the longest single prayers we pray, leading to the high point of our sacramental communion with and in Christ, eucharistic prayers contribute in their use over time to the construction of a powerful *imaginary*—that is, a vision of the world as God loves and redeems it, a vision of the mission of God and its final purpose for all creation, and the values that accompany that vision in a human life, both inspiring thanksgiving and expressing it. The scope of these prayers in the tradition to which the Episcopal Church has committed usually runs from remembrance of God's creation through fall, redemption, and final consummation of God's purposes. Heard again and again by the members of the liturgical assembly over time (since a single prayer is often and best used for a season or other stretch of time before switching to another), this prayer significantly shapes our sense of the world, reinforces our sense of the virtues and practices that correspond to such a vision of the world, and visualizes their proper outcome in the mission of God. This essay asks whether it is time for Episcopalians, whose eucharistic prayer texts certainly have their own tradition and style, to consider enriching that style for the sake of deepening their power and imaginal depth.

To learn from our full communion partners would be in service to General Convention's 2018 Resolution A068. That resolution charges us with "faithful adherence" to the rites of the Christian tradition as they have been received in our tradition, "mindful of our existing ecumenical commitments," while seeking the "perfection of rites" by the "continuing movement of the Holy Spirit among us." In truth, our ecumenical relationships are not only crucial to the first part of that resolve but to the second part, helping us toward that future "perfection" which is not so much a matter of *rightness*, but of *excellence* in prayer. The ELCA has much to teach us about excellence in prayers at the eucharistic table.

Beginning at the Beginning

On any project it is important to begin in the proper starting place. Before exploring the enrichment of our eucharistic praying then, a reminder of our proper starting point: worship has no end beyond itself. *Worship is its own end.* Worship is not intended to accomplish something, to teach something, to make a point or argue a position on some social matter or theological question.

Worship is its own end because in worship the community expresses the very outcome of redemption: a relationship *with* God, whose first expression on our side is thanksgiving. The liturgical assembly thanks, and also praises, adores, intercedes, confesses, sings, petitions, communes, laments, not speaking primarily to each other, but *to* God and before God, face to face albeit "through a glass, darkly" (1 Cor. 13:12, KJV) for now. (Even when speaking to one another—in the Peace, for example—it serves the end of a reconciliation with God that makes possible *our* reconciliation with each other.)

Beginning at this proper place keeps us mindful that the purpose of liturgical revision and renewal is not *instrumental*. That is, we are not *using* liturgy to produce particular states of mind or create particular experiences or promote particular views. We are instead drawing from the riches of scripture and tradition to render thanks well, and beautifully. For what is more beautiful than the object of our thanks: the God of the crucified-risen One, whose mission is sketched on the hard canvas of our sin, suffering, and loss, transformed into healing, love, and hope?

Yet here is the delightful irony: from rendering thanks well, other important benefits do arise. Worship is not *for* our formation, but in the process of excellent worship, formation occurs. Worship is not *for* healing, but in the process of praying honestly, Christians heal. Worship is not *for* inspiration or encouragement or comfort or learning, but in the process of beautiful worship, Christians are inspired, encouraged, comforted, consoled, empowered, and helped to envision the mission of God and their place within it. How to pray well, then, with eucharistic prayers? To begin with, eucharistic prayers should be *composed* well, and here is where we have something to learn from the prayers of the ELCA.

The Rhetoric of the Eucharistic Prayer

When we gather as a diverse assembly around book and fount and table to give thanks, liturgy works on our shared imagination by embodied repetition, structure, rhetoric (language shaped to be compelling, even persuasive), and imagery. Like all ritual, the Christian liturgy is the performance of a scripted sequence of actions—bodily actions and speech acts—which given our conscientious participation, shapes our view of God, the Church, and the world. The significance of repetition of the whole ritual, structure, and embodiment are topics for another day. Here, we focus on the rhetorical *content* and rhythm of the eucharistic prayers.

Liturgical rhetoric, including that of the eucharistic prayer, puts into motion a whole range of images and metaphors and ideas that complement one another, supplement one another, play off one another, even contradict one another like the counterpoint themes of a musical piece whose various lines come together as an organic whole. In any given Eucharist, biddings, collects, intercessions, scripture, music, homily, eucharistic prayers, and more play off one another, interpret and stretch one another to fund the imaginative capacity of the assembly.

As the most substantial scripted portion of that liturgy, the eucharistic prayer is experienced aurally. It falls on the ear of the congregation as its members watch and listen to the presider voice the prayer on their behalf. It follows that there is high importance to the presider praying it well, with good use of voice and body and gesture. But praying the prayer well needs a prayer that can be prayed that way.

Episcopal Eucharistic Prayers

Episcopal eucharistic prayers have considerable beauty, even if some perhaps more than others. Thomas Cranmer's early eucharistic prayers involved lengthy sentences of great elegance and precisely honed concepts, deploying dependent clauses that require close following by the hearer, as well as the use of doublets and a limited degree of repetition. Cranmer's work lives in a moderately updated form in Rite I, and his density of style remains present even in the freshly written prayers of Rite II, all of which (with the exception of Prayer C) follow the trinitarian shape that we inherited from the Scots who ordained Samuel Seabury (this shape is known as "West Syrian"). Since most readers will be familiar with these prayers, let us refresh ourselves simply with a few exemplary excerpts from the 1979 book:

> Wherefore, O Lord, and heavenly Father, according to the institution of thy dearly beloved Son our Savior Jesus Christ, we thy humble servants, do celebrate and make here before thy divine majesty, with these thy holy gifts, which we now offer unto thee, the memorial they Son hath commanded us to make; having in remembrance his blessed passion and precious death, his mighty

resurrection and glorious ascension; rendering unto thee most hearty thanks for the innumerable benefits procured unto us by the same. (Rite I, Prayer 1, BCP)

Note that this section of the grammatically complex Rite I, Prayer 1, an entire paragraph of the prayer is a *single sentence*. This is artfully constructed but difficult to follow.

The eucharistic prayers of Rite II in the formal vernacular are somewhat less reliant on dependent or elaborative clauses, but they continue to rely on some long sentences interspersed with shorter ones that require sustained enunciation by the presider and tend more toward concepts than images. Consider:

Holy and gracious Father: In your infinite love you made us for yourself; and when we had fallen into sin and become subject to evil and death, you, in your mercy, sent Jesus Christ, your only and eternal Son, to share our human nature, to live and die as one of us, to reconcile us to you, the God and Father of all. (Rite II, Prayer A, BCP)

We pray you, gracious God, to send your Holy Spirit upon these gifts that they may be the Sacrament of the Body of Christ and his Blood of the new Covenant. Unite us to your Son in his sacrifice, that we may be acceptable through him, being sanctified by the Holy Spirit. (Rite II, Prayer B, BCP)

Evangelical Lutheran Eucharistic Prayers

The prayers of the Episcopal Church tend toward lengthy sentences, doctrinal ideas unfurling by way of whole paragraphs, conceptual language, and dependent clauses, and often exhibit a certain reserve in their language of praise. They are beautiful, but they can be hard to follow and hard to articulate for a presider. Some of the eucharistic prayers of ELW are similar. But many use shorter sentences, are more imagistic and poetic, address God clearly and directly, with energy, and often through a more responsory structure (akin to the Episcopal Church's Rite II, Prayer C). Consider the following partial examples from *Evangelical Lutheran Worship* (ELW):

Holy One, the beginning and the end, the giver of life:
Blessed are you for the birth of creation.
Blessed are you in the darkness and in the light.
Blessed are you for your promise to your people.
Blessed are you in the prophets' hopes and dreams.
Blessed are you for Mary's openness to your will.
Blessed are you for your Son Jesus,
the Word made flesh.
In the night in which he was betrayed . . .
. . . With this bread and cup
we remember your Word dwelling among us,
full of grace and truth.
We remember our new birth in his death and resurrection.
We look with hope for his coming.
Come, Lord Jesus.
Holy God, we long for your Spirit.
Come among us.
Bless this meal.
May your Word take flesh in us.
Awaken your people.
Fill us with your light.
Bring the gift of peace on earth.
Come, Holy Spirit. . . . (ELW 2006, Option C, Advent through Epiphany)

Notice here the brevity of each line and reliance on *images*, making the prayer easily articulated and followable. Notice the parallelism in the "Blesseds," giving praise to God in a way that might draw the assembly into the act of blessing. Notice, too, the contributions of the assembly in the biblical *maranatha* ("Come, Lord Jesus") and the parallel *Veni Sancte Spiritus* ("Come, Holy Spirit") that follows, drawing the people into a creatively expansive invocation on the assembly as they hear their own voices make these pleas.

Consider another (partial) ELW prayer:

Blessed are you, O God of the universe.
Your mercy is everlasting

and your faithfulness endures from age to age.
Praise to you for creating the heavens and the earth.
Praise to you for saving the earth from the waters of the flood.
Praise to you for bringing the Israelites safely through the sea.
Praise to you for leading your people through the wilderness
to the land of milk and honey.
Praise to you for the words and deeds of Jesus, your anointed
one. . . .

The prayer continues in this way, through the Institution Words, then continues:

Pour out your Holy Spirit on us
and on these gifts of bread and wine.
Bless this feast.
Grace our table with your presence.
Come, Holy Spirit.
Reveal yourself to us in the breaking of the bread.
Raise us up as the body of Christ for the world.
Breathe new life into us.
Send us forth,
burning with justice, peace, and love.
Come, Holy Spirit.
With *name/s and* your holy ones of all times and places,
with the earth and all its creatures,
with sun and moon and stars,
we praise you, O God,
blessed and holy Trinity,
now and forever. **Amen.** (ELW 2006, Option D, Ash
Wednesday through Pentecost)

Like the previous prayer, there is repetition and parallelism in the opening lines that capture even more specific biblical imagery than the previous example, and the prayer concludes with a kind of extended invocation, deepening its petition for God's Spirit, drawing in the assembly, and artfully alluding to the Emmaus story, the resurrection, the body of Christ, and the ethics into which the praying assembly is called.

Consider another example from ELW that offers responsory parts throughout and models both brevity and the power of structural repetition in short clauses:

> The universe declares your praise:
> beyond the stars; beneath the sea;
> within each cell; with every breath.
> **We praise you, O God.**
> Generations bless your faithfulness:
> through the water; by night and day;
> across the wilderness; out of exile; into the future.
> **We bless you, O God.**
> We give you thanks for your dear Son:
> at the heart of human life; near to those who suffer;
> beside the sinner; among the poor; with us now.
> **We thank you, O God.**
> In the night in which he was betrayed . . .
> . . . We pray for the gift of your Spirit:
> in our gathering; within this meal;
> among your people; throughout the world . . .
> **Amen.** (ELW 2006, Option I)

The prayer is quite musical in its cadence. Other Lutheran Eucharistic prayers offer fine examples of evocative metaphor or metonymy, as in this excerpt:

> O God, you are Breath: send your Spirit on this meal.
> O God, you are Bread: feed us with yourself.
> O God, you are Wine: warm our hearts and make us one.
> O God, you are Fire: transform us with hope. . . ." (ELW 2006, Option J)

The work of Gail Ramshaw, prolific author of several ELW eucharistic prayers and other liturgical materials, offers a final example of Lutheran eucharistic praying from a recent collection of her work that exemplifies several of the devices visible above, and more. One is a robustly trinitarian eucharistic prayer written for Trinity Sunday:

Holy God, Holy One, Holy Three!
Before all that is, you were God.
Outside all we know, you are God.
After all is finished, you will be God.
Archangels sound the trumpets,
Angels teach us their song,
Saints pull us into your presence. . . .
[Sanctus]
Holy God, Holy One, Holy Three!
You beyond the galaxies,
You under the oceans,
You inside the leaves.
You pouring down rain,
You opening the flowers,
You feeding the insects.
You giving us your image,
You carrying us through the waters,
You holding us in the night.
Your smile on Sarah and Abraham,
Your hand with Moses and Miriam,
Your words through Deborah and Isaiah,
You lived as Jesus among us,
Healing, teaching, dying, rising,
Inviting us all to your feast.
In the night in which he was betrayed. . . .
Holy God, we remember your Son,
His life was with the humble,
His death among the wretched,
His resurrection for us all:
Your wisdom our guide,
Your justice our strength,
Your grace our path to rebirth.
And so we cry, Mercy:
Mercy!
And so we cry, Glory:
Glory!
And so we cry, Blessing:

Blessing!
Holy God, we beg for your Spirit:
Enliven this bread,
Awaken this body,
Pour us out for each other.
Transfigure our mind,
Ignite your church,
Nourish the life of the earth.
Make us, while many, united,
Make us, though broken, whole,
Make us, despite death, alive.
And so we cry, Come, Holy Spirit:
Come, Holy Spirit!
And so the church shouts, Come Holy Spirit:
Come, Holy Spirit!
And so the earth pleads, Come Holy Spirit:
Come, Holy Spirit!
You, Holy God, Holy One, Holy Three,
Our Life, Our Mercy, Our Might,
Our Table, our Food, Our Server,
Our Rainbow, our Ark, our Dove,
Our Sovereign, our Water, our Wine,
Our Light, our Treasure, our Tree,
Our Way, our Truth, our Life.
You Holy God, Holy One, Holy Three!
Praise now,
Praise tomorrow,
Praise forever.
And so we pray, Amen, Amen:
Amen, amen!" (Ramshaw, 2017, 54–57)

Ramshaw is a master in the uses of alliteration, metonymy, parallelism, and epanalepsis (the use of a phrase near the opening and closing of a passage) and frames prayers like this one with rhetorical force and beauty. Among the principles that guide her composition (shared with this author in an interview) is their regular linkage to biblical imagery; an awareness that not every prayer needs to say everything; and the clear commitment that the eucharistic prayer is a prayer of the whole church, in which creativity is not idiosyncratic or obstructive, but servant to a prayer to which the whole assembly can say "yes."

The Merits of ELCA Prayers

There is much beauty in the Episcopal tradition's eucharistic prayers. Their proportional and rounded elegance and mastery of prose, capable of rendering complex theology in a limited space, should surely be retained in some prayers in any liturgical revision to honor the tradition from which we come. But in this time and context, more than four decades since our first use of the present book, the Episcopal Church might consider some forms of prayer that land differently on the assembly's ear. The Lutheran prayers have many features to commend them, among them:

1. They show a greater use of biblical imagery, linking the language of scripture to the language of prayer in ways that might reinforce both in piety and practice.
2. They show a more responsive and active engagement by the assembly, which may deepen the sense that liturgy is the work of the baptized, while still honoring the differentiated leadership among the orders.
3. They make more frequent reference to the life and ministry of Jesus than Episcopal prayers tend to do. As I have argued elsewhere, for a church whose classical period of theological formation took the Incarnation deeply seriously as the master category for theology, we should perhaps make a more robust connection in the language of our prayer between the life that Jesus lived—his concern for the poor, his healing, his teaching—and the death that he died in a way supported by biblical interpretation of recent decades.
4. They are more imagistic, poetic, and evocative, and less conceptual and discursive than Episcopal prayers, and thus more provocative of the assembly's imaginative capacities.

5. Their parallelism, brevity, and imagery is both easier for a presider to enunciate well, and falls beautifully on the ear of the assembly, whose members might be less tied to the text and look up, watching the presider, aware of their brothers and sisters around them.
6. These prayers function less as disguised doctrinal statements, as some Episcopal prayers tend to be, functioning instead as the primary language of the assembly—that is, *as prayer*.

There are other ways in which Lutheran prayers might serve the Episcopal Church as a model. Lutherans have developed more prayers for liturgical seasons and even the lectionary of the day, linking the Word that is heard with words that are offered. While there is a defense to be made of the relatively short list of Episcopal eucharistic prayers, when the use of more than one eucharistic prayer *at all* was a new experience with the 1979 Prayer Book, in a church now thoroughly acculturated to the eucharistic frame of that book it may be time to expect that congregations hear more variety in the *content* that is built into that frame—again, enriching the theological imaginary of the assembly.

A Final Note

Eucharistic prayers are *prayers*; they are not theological texts to be recited in public. Too many Episcopal clergy tend to *read* the eucharistic prayer rather than *pray* the prayer. That is a matter of good performance, as is an illustrative use of the hands and body to emphasize and communicate the prayer, as opposed to a rote habit of some of the manual gestures we see in church on Sunday. This is not a call for flashy distraction, but for clergy to inhabit the moment of the eucharistic prayer so that at once they invest the prayer with appropriate passion and draw the assembly into *prayer*, and *with* them into prayer... to render thanks with an investment and an elegance appropriate to the beauty of the One whose life is given for us.

In a situation characterized by such prayerful ritual performance, the development and use of prayers like those of the ELCA might go a long way toward an evocative and rhetorically compelling liturgical action, in service to our capacity to imagine well the mission of God into which the church is drawn both for, and as, its very life.

Questions for Discussion

1. Where do you usually find your mind, your heart, your attention during the eucharistic prayer?
2. Is there a eucharistic prayer or prayers in the 1979 Prayer Book that you most love to hear or with which you most connect? Why?
3. Do you sense the eucharistic prayer as your own, or simply as something offered by the priest? If you do not feel ownership of the prayer, how could that be changed?
4. Are there Lutheran prayers in this essay that catch your imagination?
5. How would it feel to have more people's responses in the eucharistic prayer?

11

Rites of Healing and Transition in the Baptized Life

New Pastoral Orders in a New Prayer Book

Susan Marie Smith

Healing and Transition as Part of Our Liturgical Life

Jesus didn't come to show us how to be Christian. Jesus came to show us how to be fully human.

Like so many, as an adult I claimed the Episcopal Church as my companions in following Jesus because of the liturgy. But I began to notice connections between what we do on Sundays and other events in life. Jesus didn't use magic when he conducted life-changing healing (sacramental) events. He used normal, common, everyday stuff: water, bread and wine, oil; and everyday occasions: shared meals, walking on the road, washing. So the liturgy we do on Sunday—it isn't magic. But it is holy—to lead it, you have to go to seminary for many years and be vetted and examined and ordained. However, liturgy is also common (gather, sing, listen to stories, pray, eat and drink, depart). The sacred is both special and everyday. It's both divine and human. Hunh.

Have you ever wondered how the holy/common/sacred/divine/human rites of the church could spill out into other situations where humans are hurting, stuck, and longing for God's healing grace?

Times of healing, like your house burns down or your spouse leaves you or you're diagnosed with Alzheimers? Times of transition, like a major move or retirement or empty nest? Or both, like divorce, or getting adopted?

I want to share an example of a "rite" of healing and transition that did not happen in church, but it was conducted in the community of faith. It's the story of my friend Linda who was about to embark upon a terrible marriage. I could see it. She could, too, but she loved him; she wanted to be married; and she decided to take a risk. Then he took a job out of state—she either needed to marry him now—in the next three weeks—or give it up. What should she do?

She spoke with her priest, the Rev. Susan Lehman. Susan explained that in order to conduct the wedding in the church, she needed at least thirty days' notice and three meetings with the couple—which Linda's fiancé would not do. After a long conversation, Linda decided to schedule an appointment with a justice of the peace.

Meanwhile, however, Susan invited Linda to a wedding luncheon with other women in the parish. When she arrived, the women were gathered in the living room, sharing stories of their own weddings. Each of the women had brought her wedding photo album—all except one. Kathy had no wedding pictures. "None were taken," was all she said.

Soon all were called to the table. Thanksgiving was offered and all were seated. The setting was elegant: china, silver, cloth napkins. After the main dish was passed around and proclaimed delicious, Susan invited the women to answer for Linda the first of three questions, about their experience of their wedding day. The stories were lively. Women remembered feeling scared, elated, stressed. But Kathy's story was the most poignant. It was a religiously mixed marriage, and neither family had approved. One set of parents refused even to attend the small ceremony at the college chapel; the other set attended but sat in the back and left quietly after it was over. The clergyman also had to leave right away. The only redemptive part of a difficult and bittersweet day, Kathy recounted, was that the witnessing couple had invited the newlyweds over for dinner afterwards and had given them a gift. No photographs were taken at the chapel—it had hardly seemed like a celebration at all. Linda listened intently, absorbing all the stories.

When the salad was served, Susan posed a second question: Can you remember and describe your fifth wedding anniversary? Again, the stories were varied. Kathy's account was in dramatic contrast to the painful memory of her wedding day. By the fifth anniversary, there was a grandchild, and the four grandparents had reconciled themselves with the union, the couple, and each other. There was a big family anniversary party—and this time, there were photographs taken. The joy so starkly missing at the wedding had been present on the fifth anniversary. Linda took this all in.

By dessert and coffee, Susan had asked each one to share a low moment in their marriage and whether (and how) they had come through that. The responses included financial difficulties, suicide of a husband, being told their husband no longer loved them. The stories of how they came through such devastating pain were empowering tales of strong character, support of family and friends, loving church communities, faithful endurance.

When the stories were finished, Linda was invited to share anything she wanted to about her own wedding plans or her response to the women. You could tell how deeply moved she was as Linda expressed the power and intimacy the stories had for her, the solidarity of not being alone in her pain, the hope that her marriage would not be defined by the present problems, and the awareness that such a group of women could be available again for her and for others at any stage of anguish or joy. There was animation in the group as they left Susan's home.

Here we have a special-but-common setting: a meal shared, in someone's home, beautifully and carefully served. This became the context for story-sharing. The ritual was clearly related to the church family, since the pastor was hosting and the guests were members of the community. The pastor, without saying so, asked marriage questions that revealed the shape the women's faith-life: creation, sin, repentance/judgment, and redemption/new life.

And without a lot of explanation to Linda, the result for her was (1) to feel deeply cared-for; (2) to experience she was not alone, even in the midst of marriage troubles; (3) to recognize that what was not possible at the beginning of her marriage might be possible later; (4) that her story was part of the story of God's love and redemption. Linda came away with a new hope and confidence in the Presence of Christ's Spirit.

However, if we had a Book of Common Prayer, or even a *Book of Occasional Services*, that had a rite for every kind of healing and transition—well, even in a thousand pages, I doubt there would be a rite specific to what my student asked me one day: "Dr. Smith, can you help me figure out how to bring God into our family problem of having to burn down a house full of memories on my great-grandparents' farm?" Or another student: "There was no ritual for my grandma when my uncles decided to move her out of state near one of them. They just up and moved her, sold her house—no time to say good-bye to church or longtime neighbors. And now she's losing her mind, literally. What could we have done?"

Rite-Making as a Spiritual-Pastoral-Liturgical Skill, a Gift to a Hurting World

Rites of healing and transition are needed, and they are the work of the church. People who are part of the liturgical church family (Lutherans, Anglicans, Romans, Orthodox) are often steeped in embodied knowledge of how ritual works, and "how ritual means," as Jewish liturgist Larry Hoffman put it. Some rites of transition (e.g., Holy Baptism, weddings, ordinations), some rites of healing (e.g., laying-on-of-hands, exorcism), and some rites that can be both (e.g., funerals, house-blessings) are common parts of the churches' ritual repertoire.

At the same time, many rites are missing from the standard handbook. Churches, including the Episcopal Church, have been working to fill in the gaps (e.g., burial of a child, prayers for removing life-support). Additions are still needed; this work is ongoing.

But the need is bigger than what pastors can do, larger than can fit in books. It is my claim and conviction that rituals are desperately needed to enable human growing and maturing, both through times of suffering and through times of transition. It is the role of the churches, which have a stake in the maturing of every baptized Christian, to learn, teach, and practice the conducting of such rites with life-giving competence.

If we believe, which we do, that the sacrament that initiates a person into Christian ministry is Holy Baptism, then we need to be prepared to love and support the baptized through times of pain and passage so they can continue to grow into the likeness of Christ and participate in his ministry. And in addition to the ordained, many laypersons can grow into the competence to imagine, create, and help lead such rites.

One way to enable such liturgical expansion is to include primary rite-making principles as part of the Pastoral Offices section of prayer books. Think of the way the Prayers of the People are structured in the 1979 Book of Common Prayer: A. There is a list of prayers that must be included: e.g., for the church, those in authority, the sick, the deceased. B. The three traditional types of Prayers of the People are illustrated with two examples each: bidding prayer (forms 1 and 2), litany prayer (forms 3 and 6), prayer directly to God (forms 4 and 5).

Pastoral Rites of healing and transition could be formatted the same way:

A. Essential elements: *sign or symbol; *ritual action; *ritual words; *music, movement, flow.
B. Principles for preparing:

- care for the need of the "focal persons" for whom the rite is conducted (e.g., the one being baptized, the ones being married or ordained, the deceased at a funeral): assessing the real need and keeping the pastoral focus on them;
- separation of roles (ritual planner/leader is not the same as the focal persons) and discerning appropriate leaders;

- story-sharing and finding fitting symbols and metaphors for the healing and transition (e.g., bringing to bear Christian scriptures, symbols, words, structures like the Rev. Susan Lehman did);
- the church is made present, usually by the presence of its leaders and often in its building, and attending to the community;
- reference to baptismal vows as the touchstone;
- acknowledging the labor pains of change as an expression and integration of Holy Sacrifice;
- ritual honesty: let the rite be true, for the focal person and for all who attend;
- the flow of Christian life is linked to the person and the rite, always including Resurrection: the Christian Hope in the Paschal Mystery.

A Call for Ritual Discernment and Competence

Jerry Walker in Berkeley, California, gave me permission to share his story:

> My wife realized a call to the ordained Christian ministry. It was not possible in the denomination she grew up in; so, over time, she found a denomination in which she could be at home, and in which she would be supported in her Christian vocation. Now she teaches and serves a congregation.
>
> I have always respected her career and her vocation. I have also been a bit envious of the clarity and definition of her calling from God and the concrete way she lives it out, a way which is publicly acknowledged.
>
> I, too, shifted denominations as an adult to a more liturgical tradition which has awakened an avenue of the Spirit in me. I have grown tremendously in my faith and as a Christian. I have a spiritual director; I'm involved deeply in our congregation; I retreat regularly and pray regularly. I try to live my faith in all that I do.
>
> But you know, it's frustrating for me, because I can't seem to find a niche that enables me and everyone around me to know I'm really living my Christian vocation. Oh, I know that my baptism is my primary calling. I'm doing the best I can. But there's something missing. I want to make a public connection between

my work and my life of faith. I want to know what it is I'm called **to**, and I want to clearly live it every day, with a kind of accountability and support from the body of Christ that will make my vocation tangible and effective.

Actually, I counted the pages in the Prayer Book for liturgies for the ordained. There are fifty-five. And then I counted the pages for liturgies of lay vocations—both of them. If you count confirmation, the number rises from two pages to ten.

My approach to the inequity, after I got over the harumphing, was an attempt to be constructive: I designed a Sunday liturgy in which I would be consecrated as a Christian engineer-manager, which was my work at the time. I elaborated upon the service in the prayer book and placed it in the context of a renewal of baptismal vows. I even wrote the sermon. There was a charge to be delivered to me.

But the service was never conducted. After mentioning it quickly to the pastor in the hallway one day, I realized that our church has a busy liturgical calendar, and that we just don't—or, at least, haven't—done services like this on Sunday. Marriages aren't done in the Sunday context either. My service didn't seem to be an obvious and easy fit. And it would take some work to be sure it was not about promoting me, but about worshipping God. I suppose I could redesign it for a private service, but I wanted both to elicit the support of the body of Christ for my vocation and to affirm that all of us are the body of Christ, not just on Sundays when we gather, but every day in the world. So it just never happened.

Why was this rite never conducted for Jerry? This rite of lay vocational calling would have fit well within the current 1979 Form of Commitment to Christian Service. Rubrics could set parameters while assuming the guidance of a liturgically competent leader. For example:

1. Preparation and conversation in advance with a priest to assure the church is present and to provide accountability to the Episcopal church;
2. Making visible the relationship of commitment to Holy Baptism and the baptismal promises, either referring to how this

vocation helps fulfill a baptismal vow or including a renewal of baptismal vows;

3. Assuring that this rite be paschal—that it involve death and life on some level for the focal person. Moving to Florida might be a lark for one elderly person, and a prayer or blessing might suffice. In another case, being moved by one's children away from all the friends, neighbors, and familiar life patterns to Florida could be a trauma leading to losing one's mind. In this latter case, an abundant rite of transition could be healing and literally life-giving.

Jerry understood the need for himself, and he would have understood the need for someone else. If someone else had felt called to a profession in God's Name, Jerry would have been the competent layperson to enable it to happen. But there was no one there for Jerry.

We need people to take up the challenge of thinking ritually and extending the embodied art of liturgy to pastoral rites of transition and/or healing for all the baptized.

At the same time, there is a danger in opening the floodgates of rite-making to "anyone who likes the idea." In general, symbols are received, not invented. Rituals, like automobiles, are powerful and can hurt as well as heal—and we don't currently provide licenses beyond ordination for ritual drivers. A major leader in ritual studies, Ronald Grimes, wrote a whole book on ritual failure. Some rites don't pull off their intention, thus leaving the participants empty but unharmed. But other rites can add additional burdens or strains to already vulnerable people—and these rites should not be conducted.

This whole idea comes with a caveat: don't take this lightly.

Improvising liturgy, like jazz, requires knowledge, skill, discipline, experience, and artfulness.

Without such competencies, various levels of "ritual failure" can result. For example, I remember attending a liturgy to honor a leader of the organization. However, as a guest at the event who did not already know the person, I had no idea if he was even present. He was never invited forward; was not seated at a place of honor; was never invited to say anything. It was like honoring a virtual or invisible person. This rite did no harm, but it fell short of the goal of honoring him before all who came to the ceremony for that purpose.

A worse way to fall short in so-called rites is to have lots of words of explanation, but no ritual action. One student worship team invited the seminarians to "bow before the Lord," to "kneel before the Lord" throughout the liturgy—except that no one actually bowed nor knelt. When I asked afterwards, the leader responded, "Oh, we didn't mean to actually kneel." Well, ritual is real. If there's a baptism, there is real water, and the participants get wet. In a foot-washing, real feet are washed, hangnails and all. The laminated "loaf" of bread on the altar at one church was never touched or broken. "It's just a symbol," the leader said—but symbols are real. They have no power if they don't actually exist. Ritual leaders need to know this.

Thus, on the one hand, not everyone has the experience or understanding to lead a rite. Yet at the same time, besides falling short of their goal or causing actual harm, there is a third way that rituals can fail: needed rites can fail to be conducted. We who are steeped in the Christian liturgical tradition may have a gift or calling to make possible ritual care for fellow baptized members of Christ. Discernment is essential to know whether and who, as well as how, such a rite might be conducted, with all the ethical, liturgical, and spiritual wisdom needed. Rite-making is a holy, pastoral, life-giving, community endeavor.

And it may well be that our liturgical expertise—including our ability to improvise—is one of the gifts we as Christians have to offer the world (see *Enriching Our Worship* 5, for example, for an outline of the main components of a rite of healing or transition, pp. 7–8). When a colleague was having a difficult time, her therapist had the right instinct that ritual action would be helpful. But neither the therapist nor my colleague had a religious tradition. So the therapist perused *The Tibetan Book of the Dead,* brought a few random items to the next therapy session, and tried a "read-along" rite, but without understanding the tradition or the symbols. They did what they could, and the attempt was sincere. But rites can be hokey or merely consumer-oriented, and not even intended for the focal person's best interest.

What if someone who knew how much Christ loved her, and had the insight and compassion to see how her need might connect to God-in-Christ—the Jesus movement—had been present to have the conversation? A pastoral ritual, rich and deep, may have resulted. Megory Anderson's brilliant *Sacred Dying* (Roseville, CA: Prima Publishing, 2001) demonstrates how a committed (liturgically experienced) Christian can offer life-giving rituals to persons of any faith or no faith.

Conclusion

For persons facing turning points significant in their baptismal journey into Christ, or stuck with a wound or tragedy that prevents their growing further by the Spirit's power, the church's failure to mediate a needed rite is a failure to enable the very theology of baptismal ministry we say we believe. There is a real need for sacramental support for passages of commitment, healing, and transition. It just takes laypersons who are led to think ritually to be open to seeing how liturgy works and how ritual actions heal, create avowal, and carry persons across bridges from one reality to another.

What would support persons called to grow in the spirituality and skill of rite-making in order to pastor persons in a ritual way? If the criteria to create such pastoral rites were available, is it not possible such persons might come forward? If the possibility of such pastoral/spiritual rite-making were made available, might not the practice of such pastoral ritualization follow? Might it be possible that one of the gifts of the Episcopal Church (and other liturgical churches) is not only the offering of sacramental ritual, but the gift of pastoral rite-making skill for the sake of healing and transition, thus empowering all the baptized for their work in the world?

It is my hope and trust that whatever passages have death-and-life significance in their lives as baptized Christians (e.g., retirement, miscarriage, loss of limb, betrayal, start of mission work), the community of faith will support their growing and maturing by calling pastoral rite-makers to learn, teach, and practice the conducing of rites of healing and transition with life-giving competence. Why not? Let us bear not only each other's burdens, but let us also bear each other up sacramentally to a deepening of our journeys and ministries into Christ by the Spirit.

Questions for Discussion

1. If you were part of Jerry's congregation, what questions would you ask him as you considered together whether you might take a leading role in enabling this rite to take place? What would you say to the priest of the parish? How might you mitigate any fears or concerns that arose?
2. Have you or someone you know been stuck—unable to make a transition or move to a healing place—in which a compassionate ritual might have liberated the person in some way?
3. When was a time you participated in a ritual-like event of any kind that you still remember as life-giving or community-building? What were the elements that made it successful? Was it a time of commitment, or healing, or transition?
4. Have you ever witnessed a rite that didn't work? Why or why not? In contrast, have you ever witnessed a situation that failed because there was no rite to offer the person?
5. What did you like about the story of Rev. Susan Lehman's ritual for Linda? Can you picture yourself leading something like that? Who would you choose as your mentor or coach for making a rite of healing or transition?

12
Welcoming Care of God's Creation in Liturgical Reform

SAMUEL TORVEND

A Troubling Discovery

In 1962, the marine biologist Rachel Carson published a study of the dangerous effects of the antimalarial insecticide DDT. The title of her study, *Silent Spring*, was inspired by John Keats, an Anglican poet of the nineteenth century, who wrote of withered plants and the silencing of bird song brought on by industrialization in England. Carson's study warned readers of the silencing of birds and the death of fish and animals affected by the life-threatening elements in certain chemical products sold on the open market. There were two immediate responses to Carson's book: first, a swift denunciation by the U.S. chemical industry, and second, a growing sense of alarm that eventually reached President John Kennedy, who directed his Science Advisory Committee to investigate Carson's claims. While controversy surrounded her method of investigation, the Advisory Committee vindicated Carson's work—a vindication that led to stricter regulation of chemical pesticides.

Fifty years after the book's publication, many view *Silent Spring* as the work that awakened Americans to the environmental crisis, gave birth to the modern environmental movement, and prompted creation of the Environmental Protection Agency. Indeed, Carson's work and that of many scientists throughout the world has pushed Christians to consider their relationship to the planet and its integrity: will Christian communities remain silent in the presence of ongoing threats to what the prayer book calls "our island home" or will parishes and dioceses become centers of care and advocacy for the first gift of God: the land, water, and air that sustain all living things? It remains an open question.

More than Giving Thanks for Gardens and Harvests?

Prior to Carson's work and the movement her study inspired, Episcopalians could find in The Book of Common Prayer 1928 a number of collects for fruitful seasons, rain, and fair weather. The litany implored God to preserve the "kindly fruits of the earth" for human use. Biblical readings and collects were appointed for Rogation Days—for springtime services devoted to prayer for a bountiful harvest in the coming summer and autumn months. The Psalter, the 150 psalms included in the prayer book, inspired such petitions and collects: the psalms give thanks to God for the earth and ask God to provide an abundant harvest so that the people might be sustained; the psalms ask that people be delivered from drought and famine. There is, however, no hint in the 1928 Prayer Book that the creation and its many creatures suffer from *human actions*, no hint that chemical products or the burning of fossil fuels could threaten life.

Yet between 1928 and 1978, a relatively brief span of time, scientists began to alert the public to the growing menace of pollution, land erosion, failures in forest thinning, and use of petroleum products in warming the planet to dangerous levels. Indeed, since the 1970s, every presiding bishop of the Episcopal Church has warned church members and leaders of the peril of human-produced pollution and global warming, of the tragic misuse of the Triune God's first gift: the creation and its many diverse creatures—from bees and polar bears to flowers and forests.

Thus, it should come as no surprise that in our current and primary theological text, The Book of Common Prayer 1979, the church's concern to grasp the severity of the issue and respond to it with wise counsel and collective action are present. While prayers of thanksgiving for creation were included in the prayer book—in continuity with previous prayer books—other emphases were incorporated. For instance, the Ash Wednesday Litany of Penitence includes this petition, the first of its kind in any Christian worship book in North America: "For our waste and pollution of your creation, and our lack of concern for those who come after us, Accept our repentance, Lord" (BCP, 268). This remarkable prayer recognizes the debasement of the earth and human culpability for such waste and pollution. It does not allow worshippers to point to someone else as the irresponsible party but rather indicates clearly the effects of unhealthy actions and inaction that ask for common witness in defense of the earth.

The prayers in the eucharistic liturgy include petitions focused on human stewardship of God's creation: "For the good earth which God has given us, and for the wisdom and will to conserve it, let us pray" (BCP, 384); "Give us all a reverence for the earth as your own creation, that we may use its resources rightly in the service of others and to your honor and glory" (BCP, 388). Such prayers invite the worshipping assembly to consider how their care for the creation will affect future generations, an implicit criticism of the need for immediate gratification in the present. And such prayers also raise the question: Who is responsible for reducing if not eliminating the grievous effects of global warming and toxic pollution of land, air, and water? Is it the scientific community, public servants, or religious professionals? Or, is it the responsibility of all Christians who recognize the earth and its many creatures as "God's own creation" given into human hands for wise and careful stewardship?

We find similar concern for the earth at the eucharistic table. Prayer C praises the Triune God as the creator of the "vast expanse of interstellar space, galaxies, suns, the planets in their courses, and this fragile earth, our island home." Thanksgiving continues with the acknowledgment that "from the primal elements you brought forth the human race, and blessed us with memory, reason, and skill" (BCP, 370). The first eucharistic prayer in *Enriching Our Worship 1998* strikes a similar note while recognizing human complicity in earth's degradation: "You gave the world into our care that we might be your faithful stewards and show forth your bountiful grace. But we failed to honor your image in one another and in ourselves; we would not see your goodness in the world around us; and so we violated your creation" (EOW, 1998, 58). And there is this too: at the heart of eucharistic praise is the Word of God, Jesus Christ, the One "through whom all things come into being," the One who calls his followers to care for and defend all those things he loves: the creation and its many creatures, human and other than human.

The Book of Common Prayer 1979 contains a collection of texts for common worship that, with enlightened preaching and teaching, can awaken the conscience of the worshipping assembly to both the beauty and the travail of nature. In its commitment to highlighting environmental degradation and human responsibility for earth's well-being, it has served as the model for worship books among other Christian communions in North America and Western Europe. Yet the work to promote Christian care for and defense of the earth is not limited to the prayer book and, indeed, the 1979 Prayer Book could not have imagined the environmental crisis we now face and its disastrous effects in communities marked by economic distress. *The Book of Occasional Services 2003* includes revised prayers and biblical readings for the Rogation Procession and asks the Creator to "look with favor upon all who care for the earth, the water, and the air, that the riches of your creation may abound from age to age" (105). Meeting in 2016, the 78th General Convention of the Episcopal Church approved *Liturgical Materials for Honoring God in Creation*, a gathering of texts produced by the Standing Commission on Liturgy and Music that include collects and biblical readings, the prayers of the people, a confession of sin against God's creation, a litany for the planet, prayers for Rogation Days, a liturgy of thanksgiving for creation in honor of St. Francis, and prayers for the blessing of animals.

At the same time, the liturgical resources that shape and guide our public witness have not yet directly articulated what is rarely reported in the news: those who already suffer from the effects of climate change and pollution are vulnerable populations, frequently people of color. Prolonged drought in sub-Saharan Africa, increasingly devastating storms in the Caribbean and Gulf Coast states, and the exponential rise of forest fires in western North America and the Amazon Basin harm those communities struggling with subsistence or poverty and little political voice. In other words, pollution from chemical plants and weather disasters accelerated by climate change affect those who do not have the ability to live elsewhere and cannot count on adequate support from government offices to protect them from the misery produced by human-fueled and catastrophic changes in climate, retreating water sources, drought, crop loss, and hunger. Environmental action cannot be separated from racial justice and an imperfect economic system that prizes one thing and one thing only: the acquisition and accumulation of wealth for the individual or the corporation. Thus, in a church that has historically experienced a good degree of economic and political privilege, it will be necessary to expand our vision to include the many who are already suffering the real effects of pollution, deforestation, and climate change.

Why Do We Worship?

While Anglicans and Episcopalians continue to use and cherish a book of common prayer filled with texts, the church's worship cannot be reduced to a set of texts as if the purpose of worship were to sit or stand while listening to or speaking collects, biblical readings, petitions, eucharistic prayers, and blessings. The liturgy is not a reading room. The reform of the liturgy that brought forth the 1979 prayer book was guided by the ancient principle that *Christian worship is primarily an ensemble of actions the assembly does under the guidance of the Spirit—actions with words that are intended to rehearse the assembly for its life in the world.* Rather than viewing worship solely as a private and personal moment with God, the 1979 Prayer Book and subsequent liturgical texts present a community gathered by the Triune God to continue the work of Jesus Christ in daily life, to advance his commitment to the dominion or reign of God's love and mercy, justice, and peace in *this* world.

Little wonder, then, that the reform of the baptismal liturgy (and thus the church) asks the newly baptized and those long baptized to live as agents of reform in the world rather than chummy members of a spiritual club cut off from the hopes and anxieties of those who inhabit the planet. Thus, with Anglicans in Canada, Episcopalians celebrate Holy Baptism and its renewal at four significant days each year—the Baptism of the Lord, the Easter Vigil, the Day of Pentecost, and All Saints—as well as other days when the sacraments of initiation are needed. The celebration and renewal of Holy Baptism welcomes the local waters, the stone or glass of the font, the fruit of the olive tree, the bees and beeswax of the Paschal candle, and the cotton or linen of the white baptismal garment. The gifts of God's earth surround and participate in the making of new Christians. Indeed, how could one be baptized and anointed without these gifts?

Leaders in the early church were fond of this saying, "What has been brought to birth in the womb of the church (the font) is brought to the breast for nourishment (the altar)." Here again, the gifts of God's earth are visibly present: the stone or wood of the eucharistic table, the bread, wine, and water, the metal or glass plate and cup, and grains of burning incense. In the two great sacraments of the gospel, the many gifts of land and water, through which the Triune God acts, are present. Why is this so? Because matter truly matters in a Christian communion that takes seriously the presence of God in ordinary human flesh. As Genesis, the first book of creation, notes: the human being is called *'adam*, that is, "earth creature." In the church's worship, the treasures of God's earth play a substantial role in creating and nourishing Christians. Would it not seem odd, then, to despoil the very earthy elements that mark one's public identity as Christian?

Accepting the Discoveries of Science

While some Christians ignore or reject the findings of modern science, such is not the case among Episcopalians. This church does not read the Bible as if it were a scientific textbook: something it never claims to be. Rather, we see our holy book as disclosing God's desire to offer salvation—life, health, and wholeness—through the Word of God and the Sacraments of Grace, in the midst of human greed, narcissism, and discrimination and their power to produce misery and unnecessary death. We take seriously scientific discoveries that illuminate life on this planet and thus we accept the overwhelming scientific consensus, taught in the church's universities and seminaries, that human actions participate in the degradation of the earth and are moving the planet toward increasing warming. Is it any wonder, then, that we pray, "For our waste and pollution of your creation, and lack of concern for those who come after us, accept our repentance, Lord" (BCP, 268)?

While the Episcopal form of Christian spirituality welcomes the poetic and the mystical, these are never played off against the scientific and the political. Consider, the Episcopal poet Mary Oliver, who inspired in millions of Americans an acute awareness of the natural world, and Charles Darwin, the Anglican progenitor of evolutionary biology. Both the poet and the scientist find a home in this distinctive form of Christian spirituality. Although some Christian communities think in patterns of "either/or," such is not the case among Episcopalians who, at their best, welcome patterns of thought marked by "both/and," both poetics and scientific inquiry, both biblical psalm in praise of the planet's beauty and meteorological measurement of its temperature. Consequently, Episcopalians have rejected the fundamentalist claim that God will destroy the earth and "save" a small minority of religiously upright individuals for life in heaven. Rather, we hold that *God is with us here on earth, urging us to live into an ethic of care for other people, their communities, and the earth.* We take seriously what the prayer book asks of us: "to be faithful stewards of the world God has given us and thus show forth God's bountiful grace" (EOW, 1998, 58).

Committed to Ongoing Reform

As Episcopalians continue the process of liturgical reform—a process that has marked our common life in this country since 1789—it can be helpful to remember that the writings of the New Testament do not envision the Christian community as a static and unchanging society celebrating an unchanging liturgy closed off from the world. That would be nothing more than antiquarianism. That would spell death. Rather, Paul speaks of the Christian community as a living body, a robust organism, *interacting with its environment*. Jesus speaks of his followers as salt, light, and leaven *within society*, not separate from it. New knowledge and new crises ask Christians if there are voices and practices in their living and resilient tradition that can help them respond to such new knowledge or pressing crisis. We now know what previous generations of Christians could not have imagined: that human activity can *conserve* the earth and its rich treasure of water, land, and air for future generations *and* that human activity can *degrade* the earth to such a point that previously habitable spaces and centers of food and water production can no longer sustain human and other-than-human life. What did Moses say to a people who faced an uncertain future, except for this: that God would lead them and provide for them. "Choose life so that you and your descendants may live, loving the Lord your God, obeying him, and holding fast to him" (Deut. 30:19–20).

The contemporary environmental crisis has led 186 nations to join a universal effort to become wise stewards of land, air, and water, and thus limit their contributions to global warming. This same crisis has awakened many Christians throughout the world to the recognition that "the earth is the Lord's and all that is in it, the world, and those who live in it" (Ps. 24:1). In light of this worldwide consensus on care for the earth, the Episcopal Church, the Evangelical Lutheran Church in America, and the Church of Sweden have signed a joint statement pledging these three communions to "celebrate our commitment to hope in the face of climate change. As Christians, we do not live in the despair and melancholy of the tomb, but in the light of the Risen Christ. Our resurrection hope is grounded in the promise of renewal and restoration for all of God's Creation, which gives us energy, strength and perseverance in the face of overwhelming challenge. We commit ourselves to walk a different course and serve as the hands of God in working to heal the brokenness of our hurting world" ("Churches Celebrate 'Sustaining Hope' in the Face of Climate Change," 2013).

One, then, wonders: should care for the Triune God's first gift—the earth—not appear in the prayers of the church, in preaching, in the hymns and canticles sung by the assembly, in sacred rituals that use earth's gifts, in thanksgivings sung or spoken over the waters of rebirth, over the fruit of the olive tree, over the bread and wine, in confessions of sin against the earth, in litanies of lament and hope, in domestic meal prayers? The fundamental form of Christian prayer relies on its Jewish antecedent: one offers *thanksgiving* to God for what God has freely and graciously offered to all of God's creatures—a thanksgiving that then yields to *supplication,* to the prayer that God continue the offering of salvation—of life, health, and wholeness—in the world today *through* the people of God and their commitment to the well-being of God's richly diverse creation.

Liturgical reform is no easy thing. Worshippers become comfortable with repeated patterns of prayer and ritual action. The thought of changing what is expected and comforting can raise alarm and the fear that "something cherished is being taken away." At the same time, are we not called to consider the millions in our country and in the world who live today with the threat of their homes, their livelihood, and their future *being taken away* because humans have failed to serve as wise stewards of what God continually offers: this fragile yet resilient earth, our common home? Should we not expect that the reform of common prayer would welcome words and actions that draw the body of Christ to cherish the wondrous works of God and protect the beauty and integrity of all creation?

Questions for Discussion

1. Are there liturgical texts, hymns, biblical stories, sermons, or ritual actions that have awakened your sense of wonder and care for God's creation? If so, what are they and how have they shaped your faith?
2. What images of ecological degradation do you encounter in the news or in entertainment? What do such images communicate?
3. Does your parish—either as a community or as individuals—seek ways to care for your region's ecology and to serve as

public advocates for the land, air, and water sources on which life depends? If so, what are those actions?
4. Do you think liturgical language and ritual actions should be revised in light of scientific discoveries about earth's threatened ecology? What leads you to agree or disagree with the proposal?
5. Scientists and social workers recognize that environments degraded by individual human actions or corporate irresponsibility are frequently inhabited by people who struggle with poverty. Many times such regions or neighborhoods of pain affect minorities in the United States. Where have you witnessed the relationship between race, poverty, and environmental degradation? How might this tragic relationship be addressed in your parish?

13

Praying the Present and Future

Kay Sylvester

THE CHURCH IS changing, because the world is changing. The church is changing, because the Spirit is at work. The church is changing, and it seems wise to embrace the world we live in and shape the liturgy of the church (the work of the people) to feed, sustain, and challenge God's people to be part of proclaiming and living out God's dream.

I came to the Episcopal Church well after the liturgy wars over the "new" prayer book. I didn't experience Rite I until I went to seminary. My religious background included a childhood and adolescence in various fundamentalist churches, and an adulthood in which I rejected that tradition emphatically, replacing it with a resentful agnosticism. I knew nothing at all about liturgical worship when I first attended a service at an Episcopal church.

My experience of the liturgy was mixed. I found the hymnody strange, but beautiful. The prayers, which were composed week by week by different people in the parish, helped me to expand my sense of prayer. Most troubling and fascinating for me was the celebration of the Eucharist; it baffled me and attracted me. I stayed away from it for months, in part because I had no information to go on; it took a direct invitation from the parish priest for me to succumb to curiosity and approach the altar rail for the first time.

I fell in love with the church, with the traditions, with the Eucharist, and with God. I remained skeptical about Jesus, and there were multiple points in the liturgy that annoyed me; but, on the whole, I found that I had been starving for the kind of connection to the Divine that I began to sense in the worship of my parish.

Fast-forward many years, during which I attended seminary and became a priest. I learned the prayer book thoroughly, and brought to my parish a sense of the liturgy as a living, breathing tradition, which has undergone change from its inception.

My parish didn't start changing our liturgy out of any kind of academic understanding or theological construct, nor were we obeying or disobeying our bishop. Along with others on staff and in leadership, I sought to make our liturgies serve the parish as we are, and as we hope to be. The preface to the 1789 Book of Common Prayer, the first American prayer book, speaks clearly to this possibility:

> It is a most invaluable part of that blessed "liberty wherewith Christ hath made us free," that in his worship different forms and usages may without offence be allowed, provided the substance of the Faith be kept entire; and that, in every Church, what cannot be clearly determined to belong to Doctrine must be referred to Discipline; and therefore, by common consent and authority, may be altered, abridged, enlarged, amended, or otherwise disposed of, as may seem most convenient for the edification of the people, "according to the various exigency of times and Occasions." (BCP, 9)

The compilers of the first American prayer book, like the people who framed the United States Constitution, were given a particular gift of foresight, and they anticipated that change would come. I believe that our Anglican DNA includes a breadth of practice very much on purpose, and the current efforts to imagine how new expressions can be shared with the wider church fit right into "the blessed liberty wherewith Christ hath made us free."

At my parish in the Diocese of Los Angeles, we began looking at liturgical change gradually. Over the course of the past ten years or so, we have experienced transformed, and transforming, worship, because our worship meets people in their real lives; teaches and encourages them to see the larger story of Jesus; and feeds them, literally and spiritually. We have kept at the refinement of our liturgies because longtime parishioners tell us that worship feels authentic, less stilted, and thematically united. Most exciting of all, visitors and new members respond to our liturgy with joy and tears, telling us frequently, "I didn't know there could be a church like this."

Our guiding principles for discussion and implementation of liturgical changes have never been formally codified, but I feel confident in saying that we have:

- involved parish leaders in imaginative conversations
- hewed closely to the shape of Episcopal liturgy
- worked to ensure that written and musical elements have aesthetic quality
- invited feedback
- provided for those who have been through one prayer book change in their lives, and don't want to endure another set of arguments
- retained some changes while sunsetting others, holding our ideas lightly
- utilized beauty as a guiding principle, along with accessible, truth-telling language.

Our parish's liturgical changes began at least twenty years ago. Like many churches, we combine our two Sunday services during the summer, and my predecessor had begun the tradition of changing the liturgy when the services were combined. One year, a reading from another faith tradition was added, and guests from those faiths spoke during and after the service. Another year, we used the *Enriching Our Worship* eucharistic prayers for the first time.

In 2009, we talked about making more substantive changes. For ten to twelve weeks, a group of us met weekly to imagine a liturgy that would be familiar in shape, but would incorporate more expansive language about the Divine. We researched hymnody, talked about every movement in the service, and read through prayers and eucharistic liturgies from other parts of the Anglican Communion. The result was a three-month series billed as "A Summer of Sundays."

The elements changed or added included:

- A written preface at the top of the service bulletin about "Language in Worship": "Language shapes our thinking about God, and about one another. In planning our summer service, the worship team has made every effort to choose language that reflects a vision of God that broadens our concepts of the [Divine]."
- A call to worship offered at the door of the church, after which the people process in to the seating area while singing an entrance hymn; this hymn remains the same throughout the summer
- A reconfiguration of the worship space, from a traditional long nave facing the high altar to a "sideways" configuration
- Collects either written for the occasion or taken from inclusive-language liturgical materials
- Affirmation of faith from *A Prayer Book for New Zealand*
- Prayers of the People including a sung response
- Use of the alternative Lord's Prayer from the New Zealand Prayer Book. (For many in our parish, this was a "bridge too far" for Sunday worship.)

These changes helped to set the pattern for subsequent years of summer services. Gradually, we added to our self-composed liturgical materials and collected materials from other sources, and began to use them for more than summer worship; now, we have distinct liturgies for every season of the church year.

A parallel development occurred in our use of music and hymnody. For that first summer, we created a list of about twenty-five short hymns, some from Taizé, some from other hymnals and other traditions, that we used all summer. Our aims included:

- Songs that could be read easily
- Songs that retained the dignity of worship while offering accessibility
- Songs that people could memorize over the course of the summer, so participation became more and more full-throated as the summer progressed.

To familiarize parishioners with the music, we held a parish-wide rehearsal before we started the "Summer of Sundays." We had snacks and coffee, and sang through the whole songbook, so people could hear the songs and serve as vocal leaders when the songs were used in worship.

Alongside the refreshed language we began using on Sundays and beyond the summer liturgical schedule, we also built some services for specific purposes. Our first such effort was a thirty-minute service for kids that was inserted once a month between the two regular Sunday services. It was called "The Gathering," and it featured Godly Play storytelling in place of the readings, followed by a discussion for the adults while the children responded to the story by spending ten minutes on the floor, coloring. After reflection, adults and children came back together for Eucharist, with a simple eucharistic prayer and a repetitive sung response. This service lasted for about two years, and went away not because it failed, but because our parish population changed, and we had fewer small children for a while.

Our most ambitious "special" service was designed to follow Sunday Supper, the meal served weekly at our church every Sunday night of the year. As we had done when designing the "Summer of Sundays," we pulled together a team of interested folks to talk through our hopes, our anxieties, and the mechanics of making worship accessible for a wide variety of people who might have no church background. We called it "New Church." The design team worked hard to imagine a liturgy that would be deeply hospitable to our neighbors and true to the Good News. We massively overthought some elements and missed the boat on others; we planned children's programming during the service, because many children attend Sunday Supper; but we had failed to account for the fact that families with children are mostly interested in getting home on Sunday night, especially in the winter. We thought through the mechanics of communion for people who are on the street, accounting for possible alcohol issues and unwashed hands; we were delightedly surprised when one Sunday Supper guest worshipped by dancing right in front of the band.

Over time, we determined that New Church was serving a different group than the group for which it was designed; mostly, the congregation was made up of Episcopalians from our own church and others, who loved the music, the liturgy, and the healing prayers. With some deep regrets, we stopped New Church after three years and found another way to bring worship and prayer to the Sunday Supper group. Our current practice is to gather after supper to pray a brief evening office and discuss the Gospel of the day. It's a smaller group, but more consistent. This service is the right scale for this group, and a weekly meeting works better to keep the conversation and prayer going in sustained relationship.

The "New Church" model served us well when we decided to create a worship service with and for the LGBTQ+ community. No one church in our deanery has enough people interested to make such a service sustainable, but a combined deanery service, held quarterly, is working right now. This service is not overtly "LGBTQ+" *per se*; there is one line in the eucharistic prayer that talks about God's love for all of us in our particularity, and the prayers include thanks for LGBTQ+ pioneers who have gone before us, but the service is identifiably Anglican in shape.

These services, and later our Sunday summer services, and later, more and more of our services, frequently use poetry in place of the psalm. It's our experience that for many people in our congregation, the appointed psalms have less meaning and interest than the other readings. Replacing the psalm with a hymn is rubrically orthodox; in our discussions, we considered that a poem is equivalent to a psalm or hymn. In our current practice, the preacher generally chooses the poem, and this single change has transformed people's experience of the lessons. Our most usual practice is to read either the Hebrew

Scripture or the epistle, hear a poem followed by the sequence hymn, and then the Gospel. I hear this comment regularly from a member of my family: "everything goes together so well." We choose thematic unity and the language of poetry, paired with hymnody and even occasionally secular song, over the practice of reading all the lessons because we're supposed to. The results have been consistently positive and joyful; recently, someone commented to me, "I feel like I've really been to church."

Anecdotal reports about feelings may sound squishy and liturgically suspect; but I have to say that it is deeply satisfying to hear from parishioners and visitors alike that something from the liturgy has awakened them, touched them, or made them newly aware of what's going on in worship.

Factors that have contributed to the success of our liturgical changes include:

- The fact that our parish has a long history of broad-church worship with no particular tradition of chanting the psalms or the eucharistic prayer.
- The tremendous demographic change in our parish over the past several years, with many longtime parishioners leaving the area, and many new families arriving.
- The fact that most of the newly arrived attendees have little or no attachment to the Episcopal Church, and in many cases, no church background whatsoever, creating both some openness to new forms and the need for liturgy to assist in teaching people about Jesus.
- A growing impatience with the lack of narrative about the life and teachings of Jesus in the eucharistic prayers in the BCP. Jesus's birth and death are the focus, rather than his ministry.
- A congregation and a neighborhood that look increasingly heterogeneous; multiple age groups, gender identities, sexual orientations, economic levels, and racial/cultural backgrounds are represented, and a liturgy that is less obviously tied directly to pre–Revolutionary England is appropriate for our community.

This brings me to the principal reason we have undertaken liturgical change: to share the Good News of God's love with people who are hungry for it. I reflect on my own experience of coming to the Episcopal Church for the first time, and remember how very little was clear to me in the service. I had never been in a liturgical church before, and the *Gloria*, the *Sanctus*, and so on were familiar to me only as terms from my music history class. The friend who brought me to church may have regretted it privately, because I had so many questions.

Gradually, I learned more about the liturgy, and so can our newcomers; but there is a significant difference between language that welcomes and language that requires so much translation that the meaning is obscured. In my neighborhood, the language of the 1979 BCP has two principal barriers to the experience of the gospel: one is the exalted, exclusively male language about God, and the other is the focus on Jesus's death.

It is also important to call out what's missing. There is no language about God that is gender-neutral or feminine. There is no narrative about Jesus's life, only his birth, death, resurrection, and coming again. And because there is no narrative about Jesus's life or teaching, there is no reference to the Eucharist as the holy meal that nourishes us; no reference to the Passover, which in Matthew, Mark, and Luke is the religious frame for the Last Supper; and no reference to God's eternal banquet, the eschatological promise from Isaiah.

I am hardly a "toss the baby out with the bathwater" liturgist. I love the Book of Common Prayer. I tell my confirmation class that the large selection of prayers in the back of the book have been my best teachers in learning how to pray. If my congregation had a history of Anglo-Catholic worship, that would have been fine with me, in terms of worship style. But increasingly, our liturgy must serve many functions, because in our experience, people without church backgrounds rarely begin a practice of weekly attendance right away; they tiptoe around the edges, as I did, uncertain about precisely what church is for and why they might want to be a part of it. This adds the need for weekly catechesis to worship, and the eucharistic prayer can fulfill part of that catechetical role.

Here's an example of what I mean. The eucharistic prayer we use in Advent is specific to the season, and introduces the time of year, and the time in history when the world first encountered Jesus:

"It is our joy to give you praise, O God;
As in the beginning, when your Light shone in the darkness,
We await the advent of your light in the world;
The stars are wheeling overhead, and the year is turning again.
In the darkness of the winter,
When starlight and fire offer warmth and hope,
We once more tell the stories that prepare our hearts
To receive the gift of Christ.

The voices of your prophets echo still
With the yearning for justice;
The cry of John, preaching by the Jordan,
Urges us to turn again toward you;
The mighty "yes" of Mary
invites us to imagine that we, too,
Can bear Christ's peace into the world." (Kay Sylvester, copyright 2016)

The mandate for the writing of this article is to talk about "experimental liturgy." I confess that my reaction to this phrase is to shudder, and you may have the same reaction. I remember all too vividly an experience at a large event with thousands of Episcopalians. The event was billed as worship, but what we experienced was more like a three-ring circus; while an artist painted on stage, a disembodied voice moved from the center of the crowd toward the stage. Later, someone rose up out of the floor. I have absolutely no memory of the music, though I know there was some; it was chaotic, shapeless, distracting, boring, and loud. If something like this is your image of "experimental liturgy," I share your distaste.

My experience in crafting worship at our parish and in liturgies assembled for diocesan gatherings leads me to believe that "experimental" is probably the wrong word. I might say "expansive," or "community-based," or "inclusive." I have asserted more than once that the *shape* of the liturgy is as important as its language. You have probably had the experience of visiting another parish, or you have attended Catholic or Lutheran worship, or you've visited a liturgical service celebrated in a language you don't know: in any case, you know what's happening, because the shape of the liturgy is similar.

That said, I confess to changing the order of services for very specific reasons. The best example is the Palm Sunday service. This liturgy already has a schizophrenic character, with its triumphal Palm liturgy followed by the immense gravity of the Passion narrative. Our liturgical team asked, why put the Eucharist at the end? How does this prepare us for the rest of Holy Week? Our answer was to move it. The order of this service now goes like this:

- Liturgy of the Palms, outside
- Procession into the church
- Service of the Word, up through the prayers, omitting the Gospel (which will come later) and sermon (which is absent)
- Offertory
- Eucharist
- Reading of the Passion

There is no dismissal, and people depart in silence. This simple change retains more fully the narrative shape of Palm Sunday, and tips us into Holy Week with the Passion ringing in our ears.

Perhaps the principal impetus for liturgical change, and the possibility of adding to and/or replacing authorized texts, is the simple fact that the Episcopal Church is not composed of a single generation of a single ethnic group, who speak the same first language, who have tribal connections to the British Isles. This is good news of the first order, and those of us who have found a home in the Episcopal Church have a remarkable opportunity to shape the worship of our church so that our languages, our traditions, and our cultures can contribute to a broadened vision of our faith. You have almost certainly heard the aphorism "as we pray, so we believe." If we pray to a God who speaks all languages, who is present in all kinds of people, whose dream for humanity is that we can be one, our words and our music and every element of our worship should help us to expand our sense of, and relationship to, the holy.

Many parishes throughout the Episcopal Church have begun to work with liturgical changes in language. Though many have moved toward broader language for the Divine, it bears mentioning that some churches have attempted to revive more traditional language. I'm aware of a church in my own diocese that is famous for its Anglo-Catholic liturgy, including the occasional use of Latin. Another friend told me that the exalted language of Rite I, modelled closely on the first Book of Common Prayer, persuaded him to become an Anglican. What our parish's liturgies share with these ancient expressions is the high value placed on beauty. We seem hard-wired as a species to respond to beauty with a sense of awe and delight that we associate with the holy, and any liturgical efforts, whether for one parish on a single Sunday, or for a new prayer book, can't succeed in creating worship that feeds and sends God's people without a strong sense of beauty.

Beauty alone doesn't complete the purposes of worship, however. If every liturgy is a locus for the Good News, it follows that every liturgy should reflect Gospel values of lifting up the lowly, filling the hungry with good things, and "equipping the saints for the work of ministry." While the sermon is the principal vehicle of the Gospel's explication week by week, a liturgy that reflects the world as God dreams it, versus the world as it is, will nourish the seeds of justice and peace in the congregation.

This can happen in many ways: the Prayers of the People are a perfect place to bring to God our concerns for the vulnerable, the persecuted, the powerful, and the powerless. The narrative portion of the eucharistic prayer can highlight Jesus's concern for gathering in the outsiders, eating with all the wrong sorts of people, and proclaiming the kingdom. We can further lift up Gospel values by embodying them in the people serving in the liturgy. Just the other day, I looked at our altar party, and realized that it is profoundly valuable for everyone sitting in the pews to see themselves represented in liturgical leadership. That means teaching and training folks who represent the spectrum of the people in our congregation.

I want people to leave the church with a few things in their pocket: an experience of God's presence and love; a perspective on their daily lives, and God's claim on them, informed by the Gospel; a sense of being part of a community gathered across difference to work at being siblings to one another; a charge to go into their daily lives to do the work of love; and the specific occasion of Christ's table, "the holy food and drink of new and unending life."

The aim of liturgical change is not an end in itself. Instead, liturgical change undertaken in community empowers the church to increase its capacity for solid Christian formation, welcoming evangelism, and a nourishing sacramental life.

The church is changing, because the world is changing. The church is changing, because the Spirit is at work. The church is changing, and it seems wise to embrace the world we live in and shape the liturgy of the church (the work of the people) to feed, sustain, and challenge God's people to be part of proclaiming and living out God's dream.

Questions for Discussion

1. What liturgical changes have been made in the church where you worship? How have you responded to them?
2. Are there portions of the standard liturgies from the Book of Common Prayer that you find particularly helpful? Particularly challenging?
3. If you were starting from scratch, what elements would be centrally important in creating a liturgy?
4. How can local liturgical change be justified in light of our call to "common prayer"?
5. What changes would you welcome? Which are uncomfortable, and why?
6. How can liturgy help us to follow Jesus?

14

"What We Think Is New Is in Fact Very Old!"

Stephanie A. Budwey

O Christ, in whom human and divine natures combine,
waken us to the mystery of the multiple natures at work in every
   human life.
Deliver us from fostering false divisions and simplistic dichotomies,
and help us not to create stumbling blocks to our understanding
   of others
or their understanding of themselves.
For you have made us all one, and to you we give glory, now and
   always. Amen.
   —Carl P. Daw Jr., "A Prayer for the Mystery of Humanity"

Introduction

While it is often said that God is beyond gender, gendered metaphors—mostly masculine—are frequently used to help us relate to God. The feminist movement and authors such as Marjorie Procter-Smith helped create awareness of the need for nonsexist (language without gender), inclusive (language that balances gendered terms), and emancipatory (language that challenges gender stereotypes) language for

God (Proctor-Smith 2013). Sallie McFague pointed out the need to use multiple images for God, emphasizing that in speaking of God, "*many* metaphors and models are necessary, that a piling up of images is essential, both to avoid idolatry and to attempt to express the richness and variety of the divine-human relationship" (McFague 1982).

The Episcopal Church has done a great deal of study around the topic of inclusive, balanced, and expansive language (Bennett 1987; Meyers 1994; Meyers 1996; Meyers and Pettingell 2001). These sources all give excellent reasons as to why we should move toward inclusive and expansive language, but the arguments are often based on a binary vision of gender and do not take into consideration the growing number of people who identify as nonbinary (having a gender identity that falls outside the binary of woman/man).

In response to A068 (Plan for the Revision of the Book of Common Prayer), the Task Force on Liturgical and Prayer Book Revision was created. At the end of 2019, they published drafts of documents related to this work, "Principles for New Liturgical Texts" and "Expansive & Inclusive Language Guidelines." The latter document is a direct response to clause number ten in A068 which states "that our liturgical revision utilize inclusive and expansive language and imagery for humanity and divinity."

The "Expansive & Inclusive Language Guidelines" (2019) is one of the first documents that takes into account people who identify as nonbinary: "As much as possible it is important to avoid binaries as standing for the whole of humanity. For example, 'brothers and sisters' may exclude those who are gender-non-binary." This document also helpfully points out the limits of language, its possibility of being harmful, and the importance of language in shaping "our sense of reality" as well as relationships with God and each other. Expansive language is defined as language about/for God that "seeks to tell us as much truth about God as we can, utilizing the full range of language available to us. It does not displace traditional language for God, but uses additional metaphors." Inclusive language is defined as language about/for humanity, recognizing that "our language often has built-in biases that exclude and harm some persons. When exclusive language is used, we fall short of our calling to respect all who are created in the image of God."

While there is anxiety surrounding the issue of inclusive and expansive language as the Episcopal Church considers A068, there is no need for us to feel afraid or threatened. As the "Expansive & Inclusive Language Guidelines" state, "We seek to *maximize rather than erase language from our liturgical lexicon*" (emphasis original). By engaging in this work, we are gaining a deeper knowledge of God and ourselves, often by recovering texts from our tradition. In this essay, I hope to help the reader understand why A068's call for "inclusive and expansive language and imagery for humanity and divinity" is essential to create liturgical language that is just in that it not only balances the use of binary (feminine and masculine) language for humans and the divine, but also includes nonbinary (nongendered) language.

Examples of Inclusive and Expansive Language in Congregational Song

Gail Ramshaw writes, "The liturgy is the expression of all the people of God, and all those people need to have their voices heard. This goal we call here inclusivity" (Ramshaw 1996). As we work toward inclusive and expansive language and imagery in the liturgy, Ramshaw suggests that congregational song "is an important first step toward incorporation of imagery in the liturgy" (Ramshaw 1996). The following three examples of congregational song using nonbinary language for God illustrate and model ways in which we can adjust our language to be more inclusive and expansive.

The first is "Corde natus ex Parentis" by Aurelius Clemens Prudentius (348–c. 413), a classic text that was translated by Henry Williams Baker (1821–77) and John Mason Neale (1818–66) as "Of the Father's love begotten," found at #82 in *The Hymnal 1982*. Prudentius wrote this text during the formulation of the Apostles' and Nicene Creeds as well as threats by Julian the Apostate (360–63), causing him to be "careful to emphasize important doctrinal considerations in his hymn" (Daw Jr. 2016). Daw describes how Neale "intensified" these doctrinal concerns by translating the opening line as "Of the Father sole begotten," although the original Latin "Corde natus ex Parentis" "is more accurately translated as 'From the heart of the Parent,' an interesting ungendered divine reference that long antedated the language debates that came to the fore in the latter half of the 20th century" (Daw Jr. 2016).

This "casualty of translation" and the desire for expansive language for God led Adam Tice, a member of the Mennonite Worship and Song Committee for the hymnal *Voices Together*, to approach Carl P. Daw Jr. and ask him to write a fresh translation of "Corde natus ex Parentis" that would reflect the Latin "Parentis." This translation, which can be found in *Voices Together*, does just that:

> From the Parent's heart, the first born
> when no worlds had begun,
> this is Alpha and Omega,
> source and end that join as one
> all that is now, ever has been,
> and in future will be done,
> evermore and evermore.
> © 2019 Hope Publishing Co.

In this new translation, all four stanzas are gender-neutral, employing only nonbinary imagery for God, which led Daw to exclaim in our conversation, "What we think is new is in fact very old!" Meyers reflects this sentiment when she says, "The work in the Episcopal Church has been an effort not to devise new language and imagery for God but to recover images from scripture and Christian tradition that have not been used in worship for many centuries" (Meyers 1994).

Further, this example shows that what we *think* is tradition may not be; it might be an imposed convenience. The call for more inclusive and expansive language is not a modern imposition or undoing of tradition, but rather a recovery and preserving of tradition. Paula Barker, Ruth Meyers, Leonel Mitchell, and Robert Wright highlight this point in their discussion of mining the tradition for inclusive and expansive language:

In retranslating we need to be aware of how exclusivity has crept into the English-language tradition. There has been a narrowing of tradition with translation from ancient language. "He" and "him" repeated time and time again in English texts are not present in the original text. There is opportunity to do much more by retranslating Greek rather than trying to revise sixteenth-century [or nineteenth-century] texts that are heavily masculine (Barker et al. 1994,).

The second example is "Eternal light, shine in my heart," #465 in *The Hymnal 1982*. The text was written by Christopher Idle (b. 1938) in 1977 and is based on a prayer written by Alcuin (c. 735–804):

1. Eternal light, shine in my heart;
eternal hope, lift up my eyes;
eternal power, be my support;
eternal wisdom, make me wise.
2. Eternal life, raise me from death;
eternal brightness, help me see;
eternal Spirit, give me breath;
eternal Savior, come to me:
3. until by your most costly grace,
invited by your holy word,
at last I come before your face
to know you, my eternal God.
Hymn Online Words © 1982 The Jubilate Group (admin. Hope Publishing Company)

The third example is "Wondrous God, More Named than Known," written by Episcopal priest, poet, and hymnologist Carl P. Daw Jr. (b. 1944):

1. Wondrous God, more named than known,
    give us, firm and certain grown,
grace to doubt what we surmise,
    lest we miss the glad surprise
when we find your truth exceeds
    all the forecasts of our creeds.

2. Pregnant Silence, lively Calm,
    Singer of creation's psalm,
great "I AM" of burning bush:
    still resist our urge to push
till you fit the names we choose,
    shadows of the light we lose.
3. Save us from proud, empty claims
    in our zeal to give you names.
Let our notions be expressed
    not to limit but suggest
views that icon-like disclose
    splendor more than we suppose.
4. God not female, God not male,
    God for whom all labels fail,
Truth beyond our verbal games,
    Life too vast to bound with names:
from vain wordlust set us free
    to embrace your mystery.
© 1990 Hope Publishing Company

In his commentary on this text, Daw writes that "the opening line deals with two realities: first, fascination with naming God can become a means of avoiding the experience of God; and second, the name(s) of God are often taken in vain by people who have minimal awareness of God" (Daw Jr. 1990). Inclusive and expansive language encourages us to be open to the revelation of God in new ways, and the text here highlights that by pointing to the "glad surprises" we may encounter when we open ourselves to new ways of thinking about God. The second stanza alludes to a few biblical, nongendered references to God, including "Pregnant Silence, lively Calm" (1 Kings 19:12), "Singer of creation's psalm" (Job 38:4–7), and "great 'I AM' of burning bush" (Exod. 3:1–14). In his discussion of the third stanza, Daw writes that

> the serene, stylized manner of icons offers a helpful model of discipline and freedom in the search for theological language. The frequently expressed notion that icons are "windows" or "doors" into the transcendent is a refreshing alternative to the descriptive

and denotative assumptions that often attend discussions of language about God. (Daw Jr. 1990)

Daw highlights how emancipatory language is grounded in our own lived and embodied experiences, allowing us to see or interpret God in a way that is unique to our own particular experience, rather than what someone tells us God "is" or "should" be. Finally, Daw writes that the fourth stanza is a reminder that "it is extremely important to recognize that all our descriptions of God are inadequate because they attempt to extrapolate the infinite from the finite" (Daw Jr. 1990).

In an e-mail correspondence I had with Daw on August 26, 2017, he wrote, "The opening line of the fourth stanza ["God not female, God not male"] now seems to me to have even wider implications than it did when I first wrote it" in 1990. I do not think that he was considering nonbinary people when he first wrote this text, yet he now realizes that it can be heard as expansive language that makes all those who identify outside of the sex/gender binary feel that they too are reflected in God's image.

Moving beyond Binaries

In her article on queer worship, Siobhan Garrigan writes:

> As you sing with the faithful in all times and all places, how often have you sang in terms that were not based on heterosexist binaries—father and mother, male and female? Are you invited to sing as "sopranos and altos/tenors and basses" or just as "women/men," regardless of the voice God gave you? How is sexual diversity talked about and otherwise imaged in your worship? How do you recognize the one in every 2000 babies born with "indeterminate" sex organs? How many prayers begin only, "Brothers and Sisters?" (Garrigan 2009)

In 2016, I conducted interviews with six German intersex Christians to learn about their experiences in church. According to InterAct, intersex refers to people who are born with any of a range of sex characteristics that may not fit a doctor's notions of binary "male" or "female" bodies. Variations may appear in a person's chromosomes, genitals, or internal organs like testes or ovaries. Some intersex traits are identified at birth, while others may not be discovered until puberty or later in life. (InterAct 2020)

One of my interview partners told me how they felt excluded in church when the priest would ask the congregation to split into two groups of "women" and "men" to recite the psalms: "I'm seen as a woman, I think so, but now people who don't know me will think I'm a man . . . and I don't care about that too much but um when I hear texts 'brothers and sisters' and 'men and women' I'm sitting in the church and I think OK, you don't want me here? And I go then." After speaking to the priest to let him know that this made them feel excluded, the priest began to pray the psalms dividing the congregation into left and right.

This person also felt excluded when the priest used language such as "brothers and sisters" or "sons and daughters," so the priest would sometimes say "brothers and sisters and all other people." When the priest said this, the individual said they felt recognized, and that they were allowed to be there in the church. They further suggested that the priest could simply say "all people."

This interview partner acknowledged the recent addition of feminine language to masculine language because of the push for gender equality—such as *"mothers* and fathers" and *"sisters* and brothers"—yet as someone who identifies outside of the sex/gender binary, they felt like "now we're the leftovers." While "all other people" might not be the best solution, they felt that using this phrase was a better alternative than being completely left out and unnamed. A recent worship journal focusing on the theme of "The Whole Body of Christ" offers the suggestion of using "brothers and sisters and siblings in Christ" (United Church of Canada 2017–18). Another interview partner described the importance of being named, otherwise they feel like a "nobody." These experiences highlight the importance of being aware of the language used for humans in worship to help create liturgies where no one feels like leftovers or nobodies.

We need to be reminded of the complexity and diversity not only of creation, but also of God. As Tara Soughers notes, "All our understandings of God are partial at best" (2018). Liturgical language must maintain "a tension between the knowability of God and the mystery of God" (Wondra 1994). By being open to new understandings of God, it creates space to "disclose the limitations of our language and our understanding *and* to force our imagination out of its accustomed modes" (Wondra 1994). Being open to the multiplicities and ambiguities of God will lead to an openness toward the multiplicities and ambiguities of humans and creation, all made in God's image.

During a discussion, a student once told me that they never realized God the Father is a metaphor. I put forward this example not to denounce the use of masculine language for God (I am an advocate of using a balance of feminine, masculine, and nonbinary language for God), but rather to make the point that when a metaphor is overused, we can forget that the language we use to describe God is figurative. Figurative language tells us what God *is* and *is not*, creating "a tension between positive and negative, between affirmation and negation" (Wondra 1994). The problem is that human beings cannot abide by ambiguity, leading to the tempering desire to "resolve the tension by overemphasizing the positive," creating the situation my student experienced where "figurative images are taken to be literal statements" (Wondra 1994).

It is therefore important to approach liturgical language with the knowledge that language is limiting and humans can never fully understand or describe God and the world. If we forget that God is incomprehensible, "we readily forget the majesty, power, and sheer graciousness of God. Such forgetfulness leads to that overreliance on human capacity and knowledge which is part of idolatry" (Wondra 1994; all quotes in this paragraph from this source). Ellen Wondra reminds us that "God is hidden from us as well as revealed," and therefore "everything we say of God is *partial and limited and therefore not-true as well as true*." Furthermore, the use of conjunction, a both/and model where "God is at one and the same time two opposite things" allows for the expansion and holding of contradictory images of God in tension, such as "God is the supreme ruler of all and the servant who suffers for the sake of all."

Using multiple images of God is necessary to avoid the idolatry of putting one metaphor of God above all others, as with the metaphor of "Father." While the use of only one image of God is a failure of imagination, the use of multiple images of God stimulates "our religious and spiritual imagination" (Wondra 1994). The use of a multiplicity of images of God, "each of which indicates some aspect of doctrinal truth," also serve as correctives to each other (Ramshaw 1995). Richard Norris describes this as "disarming": "we do not give up our original figure—we use another figure to disarm it, to deprive it of unintended or inappropriate implications" (Norris 1994).

How Can We Apply This to Prayer Book Revision?

Eternal God, you have taught us to seek your image in every person in any need or trouble,
give us grace to enlarge our awareness that you live in all people without regard to gender, race, or any of the other divisions we have imposed on each other. Deliver us from the presumption of constraining you into our own image
and open our hearts and minds to the mystery of Holy Being beyond all categories and to the fullness of humanity in all persons.
We ask this for the sake of our all-embracing Savior Christ,
who lives and reigns with you and the Holy Spirit, now and for ever. Amen.

—Carl P. Daw Jr., "A Prayer for a Greater Sense of the Presence of God in Other People"

How do we then apply what we have seen in congregational song and bring inclusive and expansive language that moves beyond the sex/gender binary into prayer book revision? One suggestion is first to be aware of the language that we are using for humans; are we using binary language that excludes a whole group of people, as my interview partner described? Another is to look at the original language for texts that have been translated into English, such as "Corde natus ex Parentis" to see if the texts were originally gendered or not. Additionally, collects are an excellent place to "introduce new metaphors and images," a strategy suggested by Barker et al. ("Session One"). This can be seen in the collects written by Daw that are used at the beginning and end of this essay, which call for an inclusive and expansive understanding of God and humanity. Daw's collects also help us to understand William Adam's discussion of inclusive and expansive language in relation to justice:

> But the broader issue is the question of justice itself. The texts and rubrics in The Book of Common Prayer, if they are to promote justice, must also mirror justice. I am persuaded, as many others are, that the ritual life of a community is formative of the heart of that community as well as being expressive of the convictions and story of that community. This being so, the liturgy, while intending the formation of a more just community, must also be expressive of that community's intention to do justice. "Fixing the words" is not the point; justice and godly mercy are. (Adams 1996)

Simply eliminating all pronouns or gendered references to God is not the solution. Rather, we should include a great variety of images of God that justly reflect the beautiful diversity of creation—those who identify as women, men, and nonbinary.

Christian ethicist Patricia Beattie Jung makes the crucial point that "people can only really understand who they are in light of who God is" (Jung, "Christianity and Human Sexual Polymorphism"). As a result, a limited vision of God leads to a limited image of humanity. By having multiple images of God (the *imago Dei*), the "multiplicity of human embodiment"—female, male, and nonbinary—may also be celebrated, rather than rendered invisible (Hipsher 2009). By using language for God that is feminine, masculine, *and* nonbinary, we acknowledge each individual's "spiritual need for language that helps us identify with God, to be in dialogue with a God who fully understands 'our lives, our values, our struggles and aspirations' " (Wallace 1999). In the words of black liberation theologian James Cone, "God is whatever color [and I would also argue gender or nongender] God needs to be in order to let people know they're not nobodies, they're somebodies" (Cherry 2019). The liturgical language we use must reflect all people along the sex/gender spectrum in our communities.

Questions for Discussion

1. When you imagine God, does God have a gender?
2. What words do you use to address God in your personal prayers?
3. How does it feel to imagine God without gender?
4. How often do you come across examples in worship where God is named something other than "he" or "Father"?
5. How would it feel to refer to God as "she," "Mother," "Parent," or "Eternal light"?

15

Very Members Incorporate: Expansive Common Prayer

CAMERON PARTRIDGE

IN 2018, AT nearly the fortieth anniversary of the 1979 Book of Common Prayer (BCP), the General Convention of the Episcopal Church passed resolution A068, "Plan for the Revision of the Book of Common Prayer." Bringing together multiple, sometimes conflicting perspectives on prayer book revision, the resolution contains sixteen distinct resolve clauses. The tenth of these declares "that our liturgical revision utilize inclusive and expansive language and imagery for humanity and divinity." Even as we make our way into the process of prayer book revision, the charge to incorporate "inclusive and expansive language and imagery" calls us ultimately to embrace more deeply the dynamic, transformative quality of our shared membership in Christ's body, to experience its expansiveness as crucial to our common prayer.

I offer these reflections as an openly transgender person who over the last approximately twenty years has been in conversation and community with trans and/or nonbinary identified people—ordained and lay, in various positions and locations—in and beyond the borders of the Episcopal Church. I am mindful of experiences shared or heard among this particular, wide-ranging community, and also clear that I cannot speak for the whole. I also reflect as someone with white, male, binary, heterosexual, class, and clerical privilege who seeks to work collaboratively and intersectionally for racial and ethnic, immigration, ability and economic as well as gender and sexuality justice. I continue to be changed, challenged, and nourished by my experience of collective membership in Christ's body.

Inclusive

The term "inclusive" carries the obvious meaning of including those who are not already around the proverbial table. It is a word associated with welcome, and particularly with ensuring that those on the social margins are not left behind but brought in by those at the center. It is also a term that seeks actively to lift up and support the leadership of nonmajority, nondominant groups so that they receive not simply a seat at the table but respect and dignity, a full and active voice, agency, and authority, communal space and encouragement truly to grow as members of Christ's body. The term "inclusive" is not a descriptor of a fully achieved reality or a line of progression in the Episcopal Church, as people of various races, genders, abilities, economic means, and sexualities—including trans and/or nonbinary people—can attest. We have made strides in fully incorporating marginalized people and perspectives into the church in various ways, but our advances are neither even nor predictable, and sometimes we experience reversions or backlashes where previously we have succeeded. As a church, we need continually to cultivate awareness of the persistence of structures of oppression and to transform them with God's help. So rather than a banner of achievement, the word "inclusion" expresses part of our wider call to what the opening clause of the resolution articulates, drawing on the language of Presiding Bishop Michael Curry, as "loving, liberating, life-giving reconciliation and creation care."

The call specifically for inclusive liturgical language has overlapped historically with movements in support of people who have been marginalized by structural oppression in various forms. The movement for women's ordination in the Episcopal Church, which was connected to the wider, multipronged movement to eliminate sexism and open up space for the leadership of women, overlapped historically with and influenced the role of inclusive language in the development of the 1979 Book of Common Prayer. Rite II language was edited along the way to reflect concerns about language for human beings, particularly elimination of "man" as a universal term for the human. Additional concerns about the preponderance of masculine images and names for God remained to be addressed by future liturgical efforts, as Ruth Meyers has explained (2001, 25). Accordingly, work on inclusive language has continued in the decades since and has borne fruit in various liturgical texts approved by the General Convention, ranging from the *Enriching Our Worship* series (and its predecessors looking back to the 1980s), to the resource *Changes: Prayers and Services Honoring Rites of Passage* and the *Book of Occasional Services,* to the recently released marriage rites for two spouses of any gender. Inclusive liturgical language is meant to reflect human communities in all their gender, cultural and linguistic breadth, recognizing and pressing back against various forms of exclusion and oppression. Such language does so while drawing deeply and widely from the well of scripture as well as two millennia of Christian prayer and theological expression, centered on the fundamental purpose of liturgy, the worship of God.

Starting in 2009, the General Convention has voted to add gender identity and expression to the Episcopal Church's nondiscrimination canons as well as to support secular legislative efforts to pursue justice for transgender and/or nonbinary identified people (for a list of resolutions passed since 2009, see http://www.transepiscopal.org/policies--legislation.html). The church's ongoing work on inclusive liturgical language has begun to reflect this support as well. One way it has done so is by approving a Rite for Receiving or Claiming a New Name in the 2018 *Book of Occasional Services*. Understanding the call for "inclusive and expansive language and imagery" in A068 to indeed include this community, the term "inclusive" needs to take particular care with binary gendered language (as Stephanie Budwey also addresses in her essay in this volume). A widespread inclusive language strategy has tended to seek "gender balance" by using such phrases as "women and men," "sisters and brothers," "mothers and fathers," or "daughters and sons." While these phrases have lifted up women in important and necessary ways, addressing the long history and continuing struggle against androcentrism, sexism, and misogyny, as binary pairings these words have also had the effect of implying that gender only exists in a binary. To be sure, many transgender people identify in a binary manner as either women or men. Yet for those who are nonbinary identified, some of whom may describe themselves as transgender or trans and some of whom may not, this pattern of linguistic pairing can feel like the farthest thing from inclusive. This language pattern can underrecognize or even define people out of existence. Particularly in a context of worship in which language carries an intensified performativity (a complex concept that refers to language as not simply reflecting but in some sense actively effecting what it articulates) and the setting cultivates an unguarded, open-hearted emotional and spiritual posture, phrases such as "the everlasting heritage of your sons and daughters" (Eucharistic Prayer B, 1979 BCP, 369) or "daughters and sons" (*Enriching Our Worship,* Prayer 1) can be especially painful to hear. The wording of the Proper Preface for Baptism in the 1979 BCP is similarly limiting: "Because in Jesus Christ our Lord you have received us as your sons and daughters. . . " (BCP, 381). On multiple occasions, I have pastorally supported nonbinary individuals in deep pain after a confusing array of experiences in a single service: feeling inspired and transported by the language or music of a particular liturgy, only to be jarred to a very different state by binary language that fundamentally failed to recognize them. Hymnody too—in some ways especially more recent inclusive language efforts—can often use binary pairings to similar effect. While this language was intended to be inclusive, its impact in this regard is felt very much otherwise. As we revise our common prayer, these contexts and experiences are among many for us to keep in mind.

Incorporating this dimension of "inclusive" into liturgical revision and creation can utilize various strategies. In some cases revision can be very simple—a shift from "sons and daughters" to "children" in Eucharistic Prayer B is already available in "Holy Eucharist Rite II

(Expansive Language)" authorized in 2018 for trial use, for example. This approach simply substitutes a gender-neutral word for a binary formulation. The Sisters of Saint Helena often use various gender-neutral strategies in their Psalter to powerful effect, though in their case the concern has been exclusively masculine pronouns and imagery for God—a concern I share. Another approach is additive rather than subtractive, articulating a mixture of genders rather than a binary pairing or a single, neutral one. I believe multiple methods will be necessary and will need to be contextually specific, though in general I lean toward the second, additive approach since it bespeaks a rich, multiple gendered world rather than a neutral one. Particularly given the hard work, the history, and the ongoing need to honor and work for women's (including trans women's) presence and leadership in liturgical contexts, the more our language can add rather than erase, reflecting a textured, gender multiplicity rather than a flattening neutrality, the better. I am also mindful of the longstanding cautionary notes sounded by feminist writings, both theological and secular, about how gender neutrality can sometimes cover rather than remove oppressive patriarchal patterns. As we respond to this important call for "inclusive language" in liturgical revision, we are invited to proceed thoughtfully and prayerfully. In addition to the reflections in the Saint Helena Breviary, one guide that I appreciate is "Principles for Evaluating Liturgical Language," articulated in recent years by the Standing Commission on Liturgy and Music. I am confident that we can find faithful ways to ensure that our inclusive liturgical language "resonate[s] with Scripture and proclaims the gospel"; is "rooted in Anglican theological tradition"; seeks to express beauty and "high literary value"; deploys "the recurring structures, linguistic patterns, and metaphors of the 1979 Book of Common Prayer"; maintains a "formal" and not "casual, conversational, or colloquial tone"; is "dense enough to bear the weight of its sacred purpose"; is metaphoric; and embraces its performative function (*Liturgical Resources 1* 2015, Handout F).

As we proceed, it is also important to bear in mind an additional complexity that can attend the word "inclusive" not only for many LGBTIQ people but also for people marginalized in a range of intersecting ways. For many, the word "inclusion" can actually be an inadequate framework for taking up the work that remains to be done to ensure the full participation, engagement, and enfranchisement of marginalized people in the Church and the wider world. If oppressive patterns have structural dimensions—what the confession in *Enriching Our Worship* evokes with the phrase "the evil we have done and the evil done on our behalf" (EOW1, 1998, 19)—then to be "included" does not necessarily change the impeding, harmful qualities of that structure. In *Queer Theology: An Introduction*, Linn Tonstad (2018) strongly argues that "queer theology is not about apologetics for the inclusion of sexual and gender minorities in Christianity, but about visions of sociopolitical transformation that alter practices of distinction harming gender and sexual minorities as well as many other minoritized populations" (3). I take Tonstad's argument very seriously. I would also say, in this context of responding to the specific language of A068, that being able to resonate with a worshipful text, to hear one's humanity echoed and not erased in liturgical language that articulates—that indeed "performs humanity" in a real sense—is an aspect of "inclusive" that is indeed crucial and powerful and is what I believe the resolution seeks to evoke. Yet "inclusive" also presses the question, how will we who include and are included *change*? How can we be part of a larger call to ongoing transformation with God's help—of ourselves and of the multiply oppressive contexts and structural patterns in which we and our congregations can be located?

Expansive

The term "expansive" can begin to point toward this question of transformation. In the context of recent liturgical development in the Episcopal Church, "expansive" has been used particularly to refer to language for God (Meyers 2001, 29). God always exceeds our capacity to understand. God overflows the bounds of our knowledge. Our language choices to refer to God should evoke God's mystery, indeed God's transcendence as well as God's immanence. In the fifth or sixth century CE, the pseudonymously named Dionysius the Areopagite reflected on the astonishingly wild range of linguistic imagery with which the Bible evokes the celestial and the divine. His "Celestial Hierarchy" describes how some biblical images for the divine express qualities that may seem to us more God-like than others—these he calls "similar" images—while other images could not seem further from the divine—these are "dissimilar." The celestial can be likened to fire, to gold, to light, to a majestic animal like a lion, but these can be misleading. In fact, what he calls "the way of negation appears to be more suitable to the realm of the divine" since "positive affirmations are always unfitting to the hiddenness of the inexpressible." As a result, "dissimilar shapes" can actually be preferable for speaking of the divine. The downright shocking quality of some images for the divine can actually assist us, serving as a goad by breaking through our "materially inclined" habits of mind and assisting our contemplation (Dionysius the Areopagite 1998, 150). The Bible, various texts of the Christian tradition, and indeed our prayer can use a wide range of images to draw us close to the God who created us, who joined and redeemed us, and is also always other than us and beyond us (see Lauren Winner's *Wearing God* for more on the wide range of biblical images for God).

Yet resolution A068 does not limit the term "expansive" to refer only to God. Instead it refers to "inclusive and expansive language and imagery for humanity and divinity." It strikes me that the term "expansive," evoking as it does the inexpressible qualities of the divine, can remind us that the complexity of human beings, even amid our fundamental difference from God, is also unable to be fully captured in language. There are ranges and depths to the human, combinations of experience that any individual identity terms and descriptors can fail to articulate in their own right. The term "intersectionality," originally articulated by Kimberlé Crenshaw within the fields of feminist and critical race studies, speaks to how multiple axes of oppression can interact with one another and be experienced in complex ways. In addition to the complexities of human categories and patterns that become mapped upon people and bodies as they make their way in the world, human beings also change. All our lives we grow, we struggle, we fall short, we fight, we win, we lose, we overcome, we are overcome, we lay our burden down. Who we are in any one moment cannot be captured by any one noun, adjective, or verb. Using expansive, sometimes paradoxical, imagery for human beings can create room for ranges of experience, particularity, and change in all their complexity, even as simpler, straightforward words will also retain their important ability to name aspects of who we are and what we do. Seeking to use expansive language for human beings as well as for God can assist in spaciously rooting and uplifting us within the context of worship, inviting us again and again to be changed and to be sent out into a world that cries out for change.

Very Members Incorporate

One such image from our liturgical prayer that works with powerful expansiveness is the mystical body of Christ. Serving as an acolyte within the Episcopal Church in which I grew up, I can remember kneeling near the altar as we prayed the postcommunion prayer, offering thanks in the language of Rite I for "these holy mysteries, with the spiritual food of the most precious Body and Blood of thy Son our Savior Jesus Christ." What struck me was how that spiritual food had the effect of assuring us of our membership in what the Apostle Paul called Christ's collective body (1 Cor. 12:27; Rom. 12:5), or as the prayer put it, the mysterious reality of being "very members incorporate in the mystical body of thy Son, the blessed company of all faithful people" (BCP, 339). That language of membership, of incorporation, and of being among a "blessed company" moved me deeply. In my adult life I have rarely prayed with the language of Rite I. I have since late high school chafed against its pervasively masculine pronouns and imagery, as well as its older style of English language. I take seriously Juan Oliver's warning about how liturgy, particularly from romanticized earlier times and contexts, can form us in unintentionally colonialist ways (Oliver 1996, 13, 14). Yet of all the theological articulations of our membership in Christ's body rendered in our liturgical language, this example from Rite I remains my favorite. I love both the mystery it expresses and the manner of its expression, its astonishing expansiveness, a quality ultimately Christ's, yet one in which human beings by virtue of our baptism are graciously engrafted. That expansiveness not only has room for our humanity in its particularity but also for our growth, for our transformation.

That transformation is based on a pattern of partaking. As the collect for the Second Sunday after Christmas prays, "O God, who wonderfully created, and yet more wonderfully restored, the dignity of human nature: Grant that we may share the divine life of him who humbled himself to share our humanity" (BCP, 214). Here the Greek patristic pattern of *theosis* is movingly opened to us as an incarnational gift. As the fourth-century CE theologian Athanasius of Alexandria put it in *On the Incarnation* (54.3), "God became humanized that we might be deified." That pattern of transformative sharing is evoked as well in the collect for the Last Sunday after the Epiphany, also known as Transfiguration Sunday. Depicting the scene on the Transfiguration mount where the disciples behold Christ gloriously illumined, the collect prays that we, "beholding by faith the light of his countenance, may be strengthened to bear our cross, and be changed into his likeness from glory to glory" (BCP, 217). In that beholding we pray both for strength to persevere and to be changed, changed so that we who were created in the image of God may grow over time into Christ's likeness from one degree of glory to another, as the Apostle Paul put it (2 Cor. 3:18). This trajectory of change is mysterious. It unfolds over our lifetime of membership in Christ's body, within that wildly ranging, blessed, faithful company, held and transformed by the Paschal Mystery itself. Expansive prayer is endemic to our worship. As we add to our liturgical resources and revise our texts where revision may be necessary, the rich tradition of our common prayer very much points the way.

Ongoing, Continuing, Common

The theme of inclusiveness and expansiveness in Resolution A068 is also reflected in important ways by the multiple instances of words such as "ongoing," "continuing," and "common." In the very first resolve clause, the word "ongoing" establishes a sense of forward motion as well as historical precedent as the context in which liturgical and prayer book revision is unfolding. Historically speaking, "the ongoing work of liturgical and Prayer Book revision" signals the decades-long process of liturgical retrieval and renewal, part of the ecumenical liturgical movement that brought us the 1979 Book of Common Prayer. That process has continued, as earlier referenced, particularly through the development of new or revised liturgies, several inclusive, by the Standing Commission on Liturgy and Music. Additionally, the emphasis on the "ongoing" quality of liturgical revision also evokes the prayer books prior to 1979, as far back as the 1789 in the Episcopal Church or to the 1549 book in the Church of England. Because we take our worship very seriously, the practice of its careful creation and revision has long been part of who we are. But in addition to signaling this historical dimension, the word "ongoing" can register an Advent-like temporal sensibility, situating us within an "already" as well as a "not yet." The "ongoing" expresses continuity, looking toward our historical roots and toward a wider future, as well as a more expansively engaged present.

Indeed, following from its emphasis on the ongoing quality of revision, the verb "continue" underscores the rooted quality of that revision, its building on the theological and historical foundations of our previous prayer books. The fourth clause calls for the 1979 BCP in general and certain historical aspects of it in particular to be "memorialized" in order to "secure its continued use," while the fifth clause again uses the verb "continue" to emphasize the "deep Baptismal and Eucharistic theology and practice" of the 1979 BCP. However we interpret the term "memorialized" (and there are a range of views, as Kevin Moroney emphasizes in his essay for this volume), it is part of an overall emphasis on continuity. Yet continuity has as much an outward, unpredictable quality as it does a conserving one, as the eighth resolve clause goes on to underscore. On the one hand, revision is to "continue in faithful adherence to the historical rites of the Church Universal," with awareness of the ecumenical liturgical movement that contributed to the 1979 BCP. On the other hand, "the continual movement of the Holy Spirit" as well as "growing insights of our Church" are also understood to inspire new or revised rites. To continue is both to be rooted and open, to remain truly who we are and to be transformed.

These terms "ongoing" and "continuing" also connect with the language of "common," with our legacy of common prayer. The obvious meaning of the word "common" is "what we hold in common," how our action and our identity overlaps, is shared. In many a conversation I have heard the word "common" referenced to describe the experience of walking into a congregation in any part of the Episcopal Church and expecting a very similar experience. Having all of our liturgy in one book with which everyone is familiar has been an important part of our shared experience in the Episcopal Church, even as other parts of the Anglican Communion have created more liturgical resources in ways that have deemphasized the significance of a single book. Yet A068 calls us to a more expansive reading of the word "common." It speaks of a "dynamic process for engaging common worship" in its second clause. In its ninth clause, just before that on "inclusive and expansive language and imagery," the resolution speaks of "utilize[ing] the riches of Holy Scripture and our Church's liturgical, cultural, racial, generational, linguistic, gender, physical ability, class and ethnic diversity in order to share common worship." The roots of common worship are clearly located in scripture, even as a wide range of sources, communities, languages, and experiences contribute to it as well. Indeed, that clause suggests, without such a range of communal and experiential sources, what we experience together is not truly "common" worship. We are invited to embrace an understanding of common prayer that is indeed more "inclusive and expansive" than we ever have before.

Conclusion: Expansive Common Prayer

In A068 we have issued ourselves a powerful call. We have begun to embark upon what will surely be a years-long process. In some ways, we are making our way into waters that for the Episcopal Church are uncharted. Yet this journey also strikes me as very much of who we are. Given how significant our liturgical life is to our identity, given its powerfully formative impact, we will and we should take up this work with great care. The call we have issued to ourselves is truly an expansive one. We are seeking to remain rooted in our tradition, to honor our ties with one another and our wider Anglican and ecumenical partners. And at the same time, we are calling ourselves to be transformed and to allow our liturgy intentionally to shape us for that transformation. In all of this, we remain members incorporate in the mystical body of Jesus Christ. May the bonds of that partaking sustain us in the years ahead that we may be strengthened and transformed in our expansive membership in Christ's body.

Questions for Discussion

1. How have you understood the terms "inclusive" and "expansive" in worship contexts, or in other contexts of your life, perhaps in a communal setting?
2. Are there ways you have experienced worship (whether in the Episcopal Church or another context) as inclusive? As expansive? If so, how did that affect you?
3. Are there ways you have experienced worship (whether in the Episcopal Church or another context) as lacking in inclusivity? As less than expansive, perhaps as rigid? If so, how did that affect you?
4. Are there particular images from the Bible, from a theological source, or from a cultural source that you might describe as expansive? What might it look like for this image to be incorporated in your prayer life or in communal worship?
5. How do you respond to the term "inclusive" and some of the critiques of this word referenced in this essay? Do you resonate with those critiques? push back against them? both? Do you perhaps have other critiques of the term?

References

2018 Blue Book, https://extranet.generalconvention.org/staff/files/download/21368.

Adams, William Seth. "Expansive Language: A Matter of Justice." In Meyers, *A Prayer Book for the 21st Century*, 231–40.

Alexander, Neil. "Christian Initiation: Ritual Patterns and the Future Shape of Revision." In Meyers, *A Prayer Book for the 21st Century*, 31

Alighieri, Dante. *The Divine Comedy 2: Purgatory.* Translated with commentary by Dorothy L. Sayers. London: Penguin Classics, 1919.

Athanasius of Alexandria, *On the Incarnation.*

Barker, Paul, Ruth Meyers, Leonel Mitchell, and Robert Wright. "Session One: Panel Discussion." In Meyers, *How Shall We Pray?*, 97–100.

Bennett, The Reverend Robert A. "The Power and the Promise of Language in Worship: Inclusive Language Guidelines for the Church." In *Occasional Papers of the Standing Liturgical Commission: Collection Number One*, 38–50. New York: Church Hymnal Corporation, 1987.

Book of Common Prayer 1979. New York: Church Publishing, 1979.

Book of Common Prayer 1928. New York: Church Pension Fund, 1945.

Book of Occasional Services. New York: Church Publishing, 2009.

Chapungco, Anscar. *Liturgical Inculturation Sacramentals, Religiosity, and Catechesis.* Collegeville, MN: Pueblo Books, 1995.

Cherry, Kittredge. "Queer Kwanzaa Resources Include LGBTQ Christian Art for African American Holiday." Q Spirit. December 26, 2019. http://qspirit.net/queer-kwanzaa-queer-black-jesus/.

Church of the Province of Melanesia. "An Alternative Great Thanksgiving (3)." In *Anglican Eucharistic Liturgies: 1985–2010*, edited by Colin Buchanan, 306–14. Norwich: Canterbury Press, 2011.

"Churches Celebrate 'Sustaining Hope' in the Face of Climate Change." Press release, Episcopal News Service. May 2, 2013. https://www.episcopalnewsservice.org/pressreleases/sustaining-hope-in-the-face-of-climate-change/.

Claiborne, Shane, and Jonathan Wilson-Hartgrove. *Common Prayer: A Liturgy for Ordinary Radicals*. Grand Rapids: Zondervan, 2010

Collins, Mary, O.S.B. "The Baptismal Roots of the Preaching Ministry." In *Preaching and the Non-Ordained*. Collegeville, MN: Liturgical Press, 1983.

Constitution and Canons. New York: The Domestic and Foreign Missionary Society of the Episcopal Church, 2018.

Countryman, L. William. *Living on the Border of the Holy: Renewing the Priesthood of All*. New York: Morehouse Publishing, 1999.

Crenshaw, Kimberlé. "Mapping the Margins: Intersectionality, Identity Politics, and Violence against Women of Color," *Stanford Law Review* 43, no. 6 (1991): 1241–99.

Cyril of Jerusalem. "Catechetical Lecture 20:5." Translated by Edwin Hamilton Gifford. From *Nicene and Post-Nicene Fathers*, Second Series, Vol. 7. Edited by Philip Schaff and Henry Wace. Buffalo, NY: Christian Literature Publishing Co., 1894. Revised and edited for New Advent by Kevin Knight. http://www.newadvent.org/fathers/310120.htm. Accessed August 12, 2020.

Daw, Carl P., Jr. *A Year of Grace: Hymns for the Church Year*. Carol Stream, IL: Hope Publishing, 1990.

———. *Glory to God: A Companion*. Louisville, KY: Westminster John Knox Press, 2016.

Dionysius the Areopagite. *Pseudo-Dionysius: The Complete Works*. Mahwah, NJ: Paulist Press, 1988. Also available online at http://www.esoteric.msu.edu/VolumeII/CelestialHierarchy.html.

Douglas, Ian. "'A Light to the Nations': Episcopal Foreign Missions in Historical Perspective." *Anglican and Episcopal History* 61, no. 4 (December 1992): 463, quoting J. M. B. Gill, "My Father's Business." In *World Problems and Personal Responsibility* (New York: 1924), introduction and chapter 1.

Dowling, Ronald, and David Holeton, eds. *Equipping the Saints: Ordination in Anglicanism Today*. Dublin: Columba Press, 2006.

Enriching Our Worship series. New York: Church Publishing, 1998.

Evangelical Lutheran Worship. Minneapolis: Augsburg Fortress, 2006.

Evans, H. Barry. *Prayer Book Renewal*. New York: Seabury Press, 1978.

Fairweather, E. R., ed. *Anglican Congress 1963: Report of the Proceedings*. N.p.: Editorial Committee of the Anglican Congress, 1963.

Farwell, James. "A Reflection on the Eucharistic Prayer in Light of the Possible Revision of the 1979 Book of Common Prayer." In *Issues in Prayer Book Revision*, vol 1., edited by Robert Prichard. New York: Church Publishing, 2018.

Fox, Everett. *Five Books of Moses*. New York: Schocken Books, 1995.

Garrett, Greg. *My Church Is NOT Dying: Episcopalians in the 21st Century*. New York: Morehouse, 2015.

Garrigan, Siobhan. "Queer Worship." *Theology & Sexuality* 15, no. 2 (2009): 211–30.

General Convention, Resolutions, https://www.vbinder.net/resolutions/A063?house=hd&lang=en.

Hart, David Bentley. *The New Testament: A Translation*. New Haven, CT: Yale University Press, 2017.

Hatchett, Marion J. *Commentary on the American Prayer Book*. New York: Seabury Press, 1981.

Hawkins, Peter S. *Dante's Testaments: Essays in Scriptural Imagination*. Stanford, CA: Stanford University Press, 1999.

Hefling, Charles, and Shattuck, Cynthia, eds. *The Oxford Guide to The Book of Common Prayer*. Oxford: Oxford University Press, 2006.

Hipsher, B. K. "God Is a Many Gendered Thing: An Apophatic Journey to Pastoral Diversity." In *Trans/formations*, edited by

Marcella Althaus-Reid and Lisa Isherwood, 92–104. London: SCM Press, 2009.

Holeton, David R. *Renewing the Anglican Eucharist; Findings of the Fifth International Anglican Liturgical Consultation.* Cambridge, England: Grove Books 1996.

Holmes, Urban T., III. *What Is Anglicanism?* Harrisburg, PA: Morehouse Publishing, 1982.

Holy Baptism with the Laying-on-of-Hands: Prayer Book Studies 18 on Baptism and Confirmation. New York: Church Pension Fund, 1970.

The Hymnal 1982. New York: Church Pension Fund, 1985.

InterAct. "Intersex Definitions," May 18, 2020, https://interactadvocates.org/intersex-definitions/.

International Anglican Liturgical Consultation. "International Anglican Liturgical Consultations: A Review." https://anglicanliturgy.org/history-2.

Jones, Alan. *Common Prayer on Common Ground: A Vision of Anglican Orthodoxy.* Harrisburg, PA: Morehouse Publishing, 2006.

Journal of the 79th General Convention (July 5–July 13, 2018): https://www.generalconvention.org/publications#journal.

Jung, Patricia Beattie. "Christianity and Human Sexual Polymorphism: Are They Compatible?," In *Ethics and Intersex*, ed. Sharon E. Sytsma, 293–309. Netherlands: Springer, 2006.

Kavanagh, Aidan. *On Liturgical Theology.* Collegeville, MN: Liturgical Press, 1984.

Kitch, Anne E. *Preparing for Baptism in the Episcopal Church.* New York: Morehouse Publishing, 2015.

Lathrop, Gordon. *Holy Ground: A Liturgical Cosmology.* Minneapolis: Fortress Press, 2003.

Lee, Jeffery. *Opening the Prayer Book. The New Church's Teaching Series.* Vol. 7. Cambridge, MA: Cowley Publications, 1999.

Liturgical Resources 1: I Will Bless You and You Will Be a Blessing. Rev. and expanded ed. 2015, https://extranet.generalconvention.org/staff/files/download/15668.

Liturgical Resources 2: Marriage Rites for the Whole Church. New York: Church Publishing Incorporated, 2019.

Lutheran World Federation. "Nairobi Statement on Worship and Culture." Calvin Institute of Christian Worship, https://worship.calvin.edu/resources/resource-library/nairobi-statement-on-worship-and-culture-full-text.

Malloy, Patrick. "The Principal Service Every Day: The Eucharist in Episcopal Life and the Weight of Revision." *Sewanee Theological Review*, 61, no. 1 (2017): 145–60.

McFague, Sallie. *Metaphorical Theology: Models of God in Religious Language*. Philadelphia, PA: Fortress Press, 1982.

Meyers, Ruth, ed. *How Shall We Pray? Expanding Our Language about God*. Liturgical Studies 2. New York: Church Publishing, 1994.

———. "Introduction." In Meyers, *How Shall We Pray?*

———. *A Prayer Book for the 21st Century*. Liturgical Studies 3. New York: Church Publishing, 1996.

———. *Continuing the Reformation: Re-Visioning Baptism in the Episcopal Church*. New York: Church Publishing, 1997.

———. "Treasures New and Old: Imagery for Liturgical Prayer." In Meyers and Pettingell, *Gleanings*.

———. *Missional Worship, Worshipful Mission*. Grand Rapids, MI: Eerdmans, 2014.

Meyers, Ruth, and Phoebe Pettingell, eds. *Gleanings: Essays on Expansive Language with Prayers for Various Occasions*. New York: Church Publishing, 2001.

Mitchell, Leonel L. *Praying Shapes Believing: A Theological Commentary on the Book of Common Prayer*. Edited by Ruth A. Meyers. Rev. ed. New York: Seabury Books, 2016.

Moriarty, Michael. *The Liturgical Revolution: Prayer Book Revision and Associated Parishes: A Generation of Change in the Episcopal Church*. New York: Church Publishing, 1996.

A New Zealand Prayer Book Auckland, New Zealand: William Collins Publishers Ltd, 1988.

Norris, Richard. "Inclusive Language Liturgies." In Meyers, *How Shall We Pray?*, 28–39.

Oliver, Juan. "Just Praise: Prayer Book Revision and Hispanic/Latino Anglicanism." In Meyers, *A Prayer Book for the 21st Century*.

Order or St. Helena. *The Saint Helena Psalter*. New York: Church Publishing, 2006.

Occasional Papers of the Standing Liturgical Commission: Collection One. New York: Church Hymnal Corporation, 1987.

Pope Paul VI, *Sacrosanctum Concilium*, December 4, 1963, http://www.vatican.va/archive/hist_councils/ii_vatican_council/documents/vat-ii_const_19631204_sacrosanctum-concilium_en.html.

Pritchard, Richard W., ed. *Issues in Prayer Book Revision*. New York: Church Publishing, 2018.

Procter-Smith, Marjorie. *In Her Own Rite: Constructing Feminist Liturgical Tradition*. Akron, OH: OSL Publications, 2003.

Ramshaw, Gail. *God beyond Gender: Feminist Christian God-Language*. Minneapolis, MN: Fortress Press, 1995.

———. *Liturgical Language: Keeping it Metaphoric, Making it Inclusive*. Collegeville, MN: Liturgical Press, 1996.

———. *Pray, Praise, and Give Thanks: A Collection of Litanies, Laments, and Thanksgivings at Font and Table*. Minneapolis: Augsburg-Fortress, 2017.

"To Equip the Saints," Findings of the Sixth International Anglican Liturgical Consultation, edited by Ronald Dowling and David Holeton. Berkeley, CA, 2001.

Sanneh, Lamin. *Translating the Message: The Missionary Impact on Culture*. Rev. and Expanded. Maryknoll, NY: Orbis Books, 2009.

Smith, James K. A. *Desiring the Kingdom: Worship, Worldview, and Cultural Formation*. Grand Rapids, MI: Baker Academic, 2009.

———. *Imagining the Kingdom: How Worship Works*. Grand Rapids, MI: Baker Academic, 2013.

Smith, Susan Marie. "The Scandal of Particularity Writ Small: Principles for Indigenizing Liturgy in the Local Context." *Anglican Theological Review* 88, no. 3 (Summer 2006): 375–96.

———. *Caring Liturgies: The Pastoral Power of Christian Ritual.* Minneapolis: Fortress Press, 2012.

———. "Severance, Separation, and Divorce: Offering Healing Rites in Times of Unexpected and Unwanted Change," *Liturgy* 27, no. 4 (October–December 2012): 5–13.

Soughers, Tara K. *Beyond a Binary God: A Theology for Trans* Allies.* New York: Church Publishing, 2018.

Standing Commission on Liturgy and Music. *Changes: Prayers and Services Honoring Rites of Passage.* New York: Church Publishing, 2007.

Sydnor, William. *The Prayer Book through the Ages.* Harrisburg, PA: Morehouse Publishing, 1997.

Task Force on Liturgical and Prayer Book Revision. "Expansive & Inclusive Language Guidelines." Accessed June 5, 2020. https://www.episcopalcommonprayer.org/uploads/1/2/9/8/129843103/expansive-inclusive_language_guidelines_-_tflpbr_draft_11-26-19.pdf.

———. "Principles to Guide the Development of Liturgical Texts." Accessed June 5, 2020. https://www.episcopalcommonprayer.org/uploads/1/2/3/0/123026473/principles_for_new_liturgical_text_-_tflpbr_draft_10-24-19.pdf.

Tonstand, Linn. *Queer Theology: Beyond Apologetics.* Eugene, OR: Cascade Books, 2018.

Torvend, Samuel. "Welcoming the Earth to Christian Worship." *Call to Worship* 42, no.4 (2009): 1–7.

———. "The Banquet of God's Vulnerable Creation." In *Still Hungry at the Feast: Eucharistic Justice in the Midst of Affliction,* 50–65. Collegeville: Liturgical Press, 2019.

Turrell, James F. *Celebrating the Rites of Initiation: A Practical Ceremonial Guide for Clergy and Other Liturgical Ministers.* New York: Church Publishing, 2013.

———. "The Baptismal Revolution of 1979." In *Issues in Prayer Book Revision,* 71–86. New York: Church Publishing, 2018.

United Church of Canada. *Gathering: Resources for Worship Planners* (Advent, Christmas, Epiphany 2017–18): 88.

Wallace, Robin Knowles. *Moving Toward Emancipatory Language: A Study of Recent Hymns*. Drew University Studies in Liturgy Series, No. 8. Lanham, MD: Scarecrow Press, 1999.

Weil, Louis. *A Theology of Worship. The New Church's Teaching Series*. Vol. 12. New York, Cowley Publications, 2001.

Winner, Lauren. *Wearing God: Clothing, Laughter, Fire, and Other Overlooked Ways of Meeting God*. New York: HarperOne, 2015.

Wondra. Ellen K. "'O for a Thousand Tongues to Sing. . . .'" In Meyers, *How Shall We Pray?* (1994), 3–15.

———. "O for a Thousand Tongues to Sing. . . ." In Meyers, *A Prayer Book for the 21st Century* (1996), 218–30.

World Council of Churches. *Baptism, Eucharist and Ministry*. 1982.

Wright, N. T. "Being in the Kingdom Today." https://ntwrightonline.org/being-in-the-kingdom-today/. Accessed August 12, 2020.

Contributors

Stephanie A. Budwey, ThD, is the Luce Dean's Faculty Fellow Assistant Professor of the History and Practice of Christian Worship and the Arts and director of the Religion in the Arts and Contemporary Culture Program at Vanderbilt Divinity School. Her teaching and research focus on the relationships between social justice issues, liturgy, and the arts. Her current book project is tentatively entitled *Religion and Intersex: Perspectives from Science, Law, Culture, and Theology* and her research on Marian hymnody was published in 2014 by Liturgical Press as *Sing of Mary: Giving Voice to Marian Theology and Devotion*. She currently serves as organist/parish musician at St. David's Episcopal Church in Nashville.

Dr. **James Farwell** is professor of theology and liturgy and director of Anglican Studies at Virginia Theological Seminary in Alexandria. His publications address the rites of Eucharist and Holy Week and the theology of orders and ministry, liturgy and salvation, and the possibilities and challenges of ritual and theological engagement between Christian and Buddhist traditions. He is a member of the American Academy of Religion, the North American Academy of Liturgy, and the Society for Comparative Theology.

Elise A. Feyerherm serves as associate rector at St. Paul's Episcopal Church in Brookline, Massachusetts, and as adjunct instructor and mentor for Episcopal students at Boston University School of Theology. She has served parishes in Ohio, Rhode Island, and

Massachusetts, and has taught at the college and seminary levels for over twenty years, having received an MDiv. from Yale Divinity School and a PhD in theological studies from Boston College. She is also a member of the North American Academy of Liturgy, is active in The Advent Project (www.theadventproject.org), and is convener of the Liturgy and Music Commission of the Diocese of Massachusetts.

Jeffrey D. Lee serves as the 12th bishop of the Diocese of Chicago. He writes and teaches on the subject of pastoral liturgy and is a member of the Episcopal Church's Standing Committee on Liturgy and Music.

Ruth A. Meyers is dean of academic affairs and Hodges-Haynes Professor of Liturgics at Church Divinity School of the Pacific, Berkeley, California, and an assisting priest at All Souls Episcopal Parish in Berkeley. She was appointed in 2018 to the Episcopal Church Task Force on Liturgical and Prayer Book Revision. She chaired the Standing Commission on Liturgy and Music from 2009–2015, and served on the Task Force on the Study of Marriage from 2015–2018. She is the author of *Missional Worship, Worshipful Mission: Gathering as God's People, Going Out in God's Name* (Eerdman's, 2014) and of the revised and updated edition of *Praying Shapes Believing*, the 1985 book by Leonel Mitchell (Church Publishing, 2016).

The Rev. Canon **Kevin J. Moroney**, PhD, serves as the H. Boone Porter Chair of Liturgics at The General Theological Seminary, where he also serves as director of the Chapel of the Good Shepherd. In 2018, he was appointed to serve a three-year term on the Task Force for Liturgical and Prayer Book Revision, a thirty-member task force created by the General Convention to explore future paths for worship in the Episcopal Church.

Juan M. C. Oliver has served in a variety of ministerial positions as vicar, interim rector, acting canon to the ordinary, and as an academic and professor. Dr. Oliver has published widely on worship and Latino ministry. He is the custodian of the Book of Common Prayer and lives in Santa Fé, New Mexico.

The Reverend Dr. **Cameron Partridge** is a priest and theologian whose scholarly work centers on themes of collective embodiment, conceptions of the human, and ecclesial dimensions of social justice, drawing from critical, premodern, and contemporary Christian theological sources. An openly transgender man who also identifies as genderqueer, he has served in parish, campus ministry, and divinity school contexts and has taught in undergraduate and theological education settings. He served on the Task Force on the Study of Marriage from 2012–2015 and was appointed to the Task Force for Liturgical and Prayer Book Revision in 2018. Since 2016, he has been the rector of St. Aidan's Episcopal Church in San Francisco, California.

William H. Petersen is emeritus dean and professor of Bexley Hall Seminary. Founder of the Advent Project Seminar in the North American Academy of Liturgy, he is also a member of the International Anglican Liturgical Consultation, *Societas Liturgica*, the Consultation on Common Texts, and the English Language Liturgical Consultation. Dean Petersen has also served parishes in Iowa, California, Wisconsin, Ohio, and New York.

Kathryn A. Rickett is a teacher of biblical spiritualty, church musician, and liturgist whose faith is nurtured by the Creation and depth of unfolding Anglican community and witness. She taught for many years in the SALT program (Scripture and Leadership Training), as well as an introduction to Hebrew Scripture for the School of Theology and Ministry at Seattle University. Her interdisciplinary doctoral work explored some of the implications of narrative biblical laments for Christian worship. She is a member of the North American Academy of Liturgy, and American Guild of Organists. A wife, mother, and grandmother, she lives in the woods of Whidbey Island, in Puget Sound.

The Rev. **Susan Marie Smith** earned her PhD in Worship, Proclamation, and the Arts at the Graduate Theological Union (Berkeley, California) and taught at St. Paul (United Methodist) School of Theology (Kansas City, Missouri). An Episcopal priest, she also served as chaplain at St.

Andrew's School (Saratoga, California), rector at St. Alban's Church (Bexley, Ohio), and priest-in-charge at Church of the Nativity Episcopal (Indianapolis, Indiana). Her work, focused on baptismal ecclesiology and pastoral ritual, has been both academic and practical, enabling the creation of numerous personal rites of healing and transition.

The Rev. **Sylvia Sweeney**, PhD, retired as dean and president of Bloy House, the Episcopal Theological School at Los Angeles where she continues to teach liturgics and homiletics. Before coming to Bloy House in 2009, she was a parish priest in congregations in Montana, Idaho, and California. She is the author of *Ecofeminist Perspective on Ash Wednesday and Lent* (Peter Lang Publishing, 2009) and *Winged with Longing for Better Things* (Church Publishing, 2019). A core theme of her teaching and writing is how a well-developed twenty-first-century baptismally centered theology of the church offers essential common ground for conversation and cooperation between scholars and (lay and ordained) ministers.

The Rev. **Kay Sylvester** is the rector of St. Paul's Episcopal Church in Tustin, California, in the Diocese of Los Angeles. She is part of the planning team for worship at Diocesan Convention and Clergy Conference, a member of the Standing Committee, and a mentor for the diocesan "discernment year" for people exploring vocation. In real life, she is owned by two cats, and has too many guitars.

The Rev. **Samuel Torvend**, PhD, is senior historian in the Department of Religion at Pacific Lutheran University and associate priest for adult formation at Christ Episcopal Church in Tacoma, Washington. He has served as professor of liturgy at the University of St. Thomas (St. Paul, Minnesota) and Aquinas Institute (St. Louis, Missouri). Fr. Torvend is chair emeritus and current member of the Commission on Liturgy and the Arts in the Diocese of Olympia, and is a member of the Ecology and Liturgy Seminar of the North American Academy of Liturgy.

In a teaching ministry that has lasted over a half-century, **Louis Weil** has served as a member of the faculties of three Episcopal seminaries, in

Puerto Rico, Wisconsin, and last in California at the Church Divinity School of the Pacific, where he held the Hodges-Haynes Chair in Liturgics from 1999 until 2009. His work as a teacher of liturgical studies led to his teaching on five continents, and to his participation in ecumenical programs with Roman Catholic, Lutheran, and Reformed scholars. Weil earned his doctorate in liturgical studies at the Catholic University of Paris in 1972. He has authored several books in his field, including *Sacraments and Liturgy: The Outward Sign* (1983) and *Liturgical Sense: The Logic of Rite* (2013). In addition to his books, Weil authored about one hundred articles on a wide range of sacramental and liturgical subjects.

www.ingramcontent.com/pod-product-compliance
Ingram Content Group UK Ltd.
Pitfield, Milton Keynes, MK11 3LW, UK
UKHW021846140426
5217IPUK00022B/1608